After the Coup

After the Coup

An Ethnographic Reframing
of Guatemala 1954

Edited by
**TIMOTHY J. SMITH AND
ABIGAIL E. ADAMS**

UNIVERSITY OF ILLINOIS PRESS
Urbana, Chicago, and Springfield

© 2011 by the Board of Trustees
of the University of Illinois
All rights reserved
Manufactured in the United States of America
1 2 3 4 5 C P 5 4 3 2 1
∞ This book is printed on acid-free paper.

Library of Congress Cataloging-in-Publication Data
After the coup : an ethnographic reframing of Guatemala, 1954 /
edited by Timothy J. Smith and Abigail E. Adams.
    p.   cm.
Includes index.
ISBN 978-0-252-07784-5 (acid-free paper)
ISBN 978-0-252-03586-9 (acid-free paper)
1. Guatemala—History—Revolution, 1954.
2. Guatemala—History—Revolution, 1954—Influence.
3. Ethnology—Guatemala. 4. Guatemala—Ethnic relations.
5. Mayas—Violence against—Guatemala—History—
20th century. 6. Guatemala—History—1945–1985.
7. Guatemala—History—1985– . 8. Guatemala—Politics
and government—1945–1985. 9. Guatemala—Politics and
government—1985– . I. Smith, Timothy J., 1957– .
II. Adams, Abigail E.
F1466.5.A47   2010
972.8105′2—dc22   2010049187

To June and Rick

Thank you for inspiring
generations of anthropologists

Thank you for inspiring
communities of scholars

Matyöx chiwe, qate' qatata'

Contents

Acknowledgments

We are very grateful to the University of Illinois at Urbana-Champaign (UIUC) for sponsoring the April 2005 conference that formed the basis for this book: "From a Springtime of Democracy to a Winter of Cold War: The 1954 Guatemalan Coup and Its Lasting Impact on U.S./Latin American Relations." In particular, we would like to thank Dr. Nils Jacobson, who was the director of the Center for Latin American and Caribbean Studies (CLACS) at the time. The Center for Latin American Studies at the University of Chicago, the consortium partner of UIUC-CLACS, was also vital to this academic undertaking. Abigail Adams maintained painstaking correspondence and diligent lines of communication to bring our colleagues together. Timothy Smith, who was the associate director of CLACS at the time, secured funding for this event from three major sources at UIUC: the International Council, which awarded CLACS a William and Flora Hewlett International Conference Grant; the Center for Advanced Study and the George A. Miller Programs Committee for a Public Events Grant; and the College of Liberal Arts and Sciences for a State of the Art Conference Grant.

Other units at UIUC were instrumental in their support: Center for Global Studies; Department of Anthropology; Department of Geography; Department of History; Department of Political Science; Department of Sociology; Illinois Program for Research in the Humanities; International Programs and Studies; Latina/Latino Studies Program; Office of the Chancellor; Program in Arms Control, Disarmament, and International Security; Women and Gender in Global Perspectives Program; and Amnesty International UIUC-Chapter. At the University of Illinois, we would like to thank Norman

Whitten, Alejandro Lugo, Andrew Orta, Arlene Torres, Paul Garber, Larry Mann, Earl Kellogg, Matti Bunzl, Matt Rosenstein, Edward Kolodziej, Peter Fritzsche, Gale Summerfield, Tim Liao, and Charles Stewart. We want to also thank the University of Illinois Press and Joan Catapano for being patient and for working with us to see this volume published, and Copenhaver Cumpston and Paula Newcomb for artistic direction. Our special thanks go out to Michael Stone, David Stoll, Edward Fischer, and an anonymous reviewer for their insightful comments and suggestions over the life of this process.

We are grateful to our two discussants for the conference, John Watanabe and Zachary Elkins, and conference participant Diane M. Nelson, whose paper appears in *Reckoning: The Ends of War in Guatemala* (Duke University Press, 2009).

External to the university, we finally thank the U.S. Department of Education and the U.S. Embassy in Guatemala for helping bring to Champaign Victor Montejo, who was serving as the secretary of peace in the presidency of the Republic of Guatemala. Finally, we thank Anthony Calamai and Gregory Reck at Appalachian State University for allocating funds for image reproduction.

Timothy J. Smith
Abigail E. Adams

After the Coup

Reflecting upon the Historical Impact of the Coup

TIMOTHY J. SMITH

In 1954, leaders of a coup overthrew the democratically elected president, Jacobo Arbenz Guzmán, and ended Guatemala's so-called Diez Años de Primavera (Ten Years of Spring), the 1944–54 decade of progressive legislation inspired in part by Franklin D. Roosevelt's New Deal. Guatemala 1954 represented the U.S. government's first covert action in Latin America and its second overthrow of a foreign government, after August 1953's coup removed Iranian Prime Minister Mohammad Mosaddegh. Many scholars have detailed the events leading to the 1954 coup and the rationale for U.S. involvement, as well as the aftermath (see for example Sinclair 1995; Handy 1984, 1988, 1990, 1994; Gleijeses 1991; Grandin 2000, 2004; Wilkinson 2002; Schlesinger and Kinzer 1982; Immerman 1982; Aybar de Soto 1978). But the coup also radically changed the relationship between U.S. and Guatemalan social scientists, who are, in the words of anthropologist Richard Adams, another set of professional interveners. In particular, this major event has shaped either directly or indirectly the U.S.-based anthropologists and their projects in Guatemala to the present.

This book results from the only major academic-based conference on the half-century anniversary of Guatemala 1954's aftermath, hosted by the University of Illinois at Urbana-Champaign in 2005. Participants engaged in critical ethnographic reflection on the historical impact of the coup, work heightened by two recent actions of the U.S. government: its repeated interventions in other countries during the George W. Bush administration with little planning for highly problematic consequences; and its release of declassified documents concerning Guatemala 1954 in 1997 and 2003. These scholars focused upon two guiding queries: "What can U.S.-based ethnography offer to an analysis of 1954, beyond merely invoking or confirming explanations from historians, journalists, or political scientists?" and "To what extent have anthropologists in the United States been affected by 1954, given their presence in Guatemala at and after the time of the coup?"

The authors assembled in this volume do not merely read Guatemala's history through the events that link the U.S.-based researcher to the Guatemalan subject. Rather, their intent is to survey how the coup has fit into ethnographic representations of Guatemala, and how ethnographers provide an understanding of how the events preceding and following the coup played out in communities and in vastly different regions of the country, paying heed to the voices of individuals with whom we have lived and worked.

Writing from the Shadow of Guatemala 1954

Reviewing dozens of U.S.-produced ethnographies of Guatemala from the 1950s forward, the editors find many that provide little to no historical context concerning 1954. It appears de rigueur to give a nod to the impact of 1871's liberal revolution and the loss of land and labor rights for Maya communities, as well as the counterinsurgency of the 1970s and 1980s. However, the 1944–54 period and coup aftermath receive varying degrees of attention. Several studies cover the colonial era, jump to the late 1800s, and then skip to the violence beginning in the late 1970s, perhaps glancing at the 1960s.

Three interesting trends appeared in the ethnographies revisited, whose authors mention the coup: a) the exclusive description of the coup as CIA- or U.S.-enacted; b) the description of the coup as either ending or beginning certain histories, rather than a major event in longer durées of social-historical developments; and c) the documentation of one or more of those very sociohistorical developments in their ethnography, despite their invocation of either trope a or b above.

The first tendency (not universal, as we demonstrate) is to invoke the boilerplate that connects the Central Intelligence Agency (CIA), Arbenz's land reform and the threatened United Fruit Company, the beginning of cold war–infused U.S. intervention, and the continued marginalization of Guatemalan Mayas. The text usually reads like this: "Arbenz's agrarian reforms and suspected collusion with communists upset the United States government and the United Fruit Company, which in turn prompted the brothers John Foster Dulles (U.S. secretary of state) and Allen Welsh Dulles (U.S. director of the Central Intelligence Agency; board member of the United Fruit Company) to oust the democratically elected president of Guatemala."

The most marked signifier of this first trend is the hyphenated descriptor of 1954—CIA-backed, CIA-engineered, CIA-orchestrated, U.S.-backed, U.S.-sponsored—or statements such as "'my' government had overthrown democratically elected governments" or "a civilian government redistributing land was overthrown by the U.S. Central Intelligence Agency" (all culled from recent U.S.-based ethnographies of Guatemala: Fischer 1996: 53; 2001: 75; Green 1999: 34; Manz 2004: 49, 78; Montejo 2005: 115, 1999: 38; Nelson 1999: 51; 2009: xix; Stoll 1993: 14, 42; Warren 1989: 13). Anthropologists are far from the only writers and scholars who use the hyphenated branding of the coup, usually as a well-intended solidarity-minded reflexive turn. However, we argue that to so heavily give weight to the United States, even given its decisive implication, reduces the coup to a U.S.-Guatemalan conflict and downplays the role of local and national actors in Guatemala.

Many ethnographers break from the above boilerplate in their discussions of the 1944–54 period and address other concerns. These ethnographers tend to display the second trend, the treatment of the coup as the alpha or omega for understanding Guatemalan social relations since the midcentury. As the omega, the coup is viewed as the end of the Ten Years of Spring, which was characterized by the social reforms implemented by the Arévalo and Arbenz administrations, the revolutionary committees, and the agrarian and labor reforms (although as Wasserstrom noted in 1975, very few ethnographers have analyzed the impact of the land reforms on the community of their study, but there are some shining standouts noted below). As the alpha, the coup prompts the rise of successive military dictatorships, either as a continuity beginning with Carlos Castillo Armas and peaking with the counterinsurgency of Fernando Romeo Lucas García and José Efraín Ríos Montt, or more indirectly, by providing an impetus to military officers hardened after 1959 Cuba and the 1962–63 revolutionary uprising sparked by their disaffected brethren (Adams 1988: 290–291, 1990: 158; Stoll 1993: 15); the opening of Central America's location in U.S. cold war territorial hegemony (Fischer 2001: 75, 92; Montejo 2005: 96, 115; Nelson 2009: 327n3; Carmack 1988: ix; Manz 2004: 21); the opening of covert CIA presence in the region; the beginnings of Latin American armed radicalism, either directly through a loss of "faith in peaceful, legal, and reformist methods of social change" (C. Smith 1990: 264) or indirectly through the initial formation of the 1962–63 guerrilla movement by disaffected army officers. Indeed, the majority of U.S.-based anthropologists have drawn a direct link between the coup and the thirty-six-year armed conflict that ended in 1996.

"No Single Cut": 1954, Context, and Ethnographic Contributions

As Diane Nelson points out, "No single cut began or ended the war" (2009: 74). Many factors contributed to the later *violencia* that scarred late-twentieth-century Guatemala. In line with Nelson's counsel, the final trend noted by the editors is that—despite invoking either or both of the tropes described above—the ethnographers who elaborate on the coup reveal more complex pictures of coup supporters and leaders, and of the coup's historical context and social developments. Several U.S.-based ethnographies take important steps in the scholarship of the broader 1944–54 period, toward creating alternative understandings to the top-down CIA–United Fruit Company metanarrative. While they have the "CIA-backed" tagline somewhere in their pages, these ethnographies tell a story of community interests, the Roman Catholic Church and "anticommunism," *indigenista* philosophies and education, generational conflicts, sociopolitical awakenings, indigenous identity, electoral politics, Protestant missions, and memory. In fact, we find four major themes that serve to frame anthropological accounts of the period shortly before and after the coup.

THE ROMAN CATHOLIC CHURCH AND COMMUNISM: PROVIDENTIAL MISSIONS

Several ethnographies detail the escalation of critical conflicts with the Guatemalan Roman Catholic Church, beginning with Juan José Arévalo's administration. Despite his initial openness toward foreign missionaries (allowing the Missouri Synod Lutherans and Southern Baptists into the country), Arévalo upheld the inclusion of Jorge Ubico y Castañeda's anticlerical legislation in the constitution of 1945, which prohibited direct involvement of religious groups in politics or organized labor. Ubico is remembered for leniency toward religious missionaries as long as they refrained from political commentary or activity. But for Arévalo, a similar policy led to increased hostility between the Catholic Church and the state (Warren 1989: 87).

Hostility was not the case everywhere, however. Robert Carmack describes a close relationship between the Guatemalan founder of Catholic Action in Momostenango, Monsignor Rafael Gonzalez, and Arévalo. Carmack argues that it was precisely because of the anticlerical legislation (simultaneous with the government's promotion of religious freedom) and the church's decision to "officially" keep out of political affairs, that the Catholic Church was able to "launch religious reform on a grand scale." He writes that "the monsignor's ideas for modernizing the thinking of the Indians were consistent with revolutionary policies of the time" (1995: 227–228).

Several anthropologists describe how tensions between state and church sharpened under Arbenz (Green 1999: 44; Warren 1989: 151–154). Kay Warren attributes the opposition to Arbenz and his reforms that she heard expressed by many sectors of San Andrés Semetebaj to the reach of the Catholic Church's negative portrayal; Archbishop Mariano Rossell y Arellano preached that the revolutionary agenda was "communism" and incompatible with the religious priorities of Catholicism. At the same time, the introduction of the catechist movement Catholic Action into the countryside was also part of the overall "sociological awakening" described below, an awakening that formed part of the democratic openings of the Ten Years of Spring (Warren 1989; Fischer 2001: 89–90; Adams 1957, 1988, 1990).

In a move to include rural populations in a more inclusive socioeconomic block, Arbenz looked to modernize the education system by training teachers in indigenous communities. Missionaries with Wycliffe Bible Translators (predecessor to the Summer Institute of Linguistics) were able to circumvent antiforeigner restrictions by offering their assistance. Arbenz relied on the Summer Institute of Linguistics as a viable partner to increase literacy among indigenous populations by supplying textbooks, training teachers, and establishing standards for Mayan language orthographies (Fischer 2001: 89–90).

The anticlerical policies that had soured the relationship between the Catholic Church and the revolutionary governments ended with the arrival of Castillo Armas, who embraced Catholics as allies. With a new legal status and privileges granted to it by the counterrevolutionary government in the 1956 constitution (i.e., ability to acquire and own property, ability to perform civil marriages, support for religious education, etc.), the Catholic Church focused on young Indians who had been involved in the politics and committees of the Arévalo and Arbenz years. Indians found new opportunities with the church's postcoup social programs to participate in national life through local grassroots organizations and educational programs. This included the establishment of boarding schools (indigenous institutes) by Archbishop Rossell y Arellano. Victor Montejo describes the archbishop's actions as "a measure to stop Maya from falling into the traps of Communist manipulation," arguing that some of the earliest forms of Pan-Mayanism developed in the new institutes (2005: 74).

Maya cultural activism would not appear on the public stage for another twenty years. The armed revolution of the 1960s made it impossible for the Mayas to participate in anything seen as political or subversive. Only by the late 1960s did activists openly pursue their demands again (albeit selectively and strategically in the form of linguistic activism), which led to a renewed interest in Mayan languages and linguistic rights legislation in the 1970s (Fischer 2001: 92; cf. Warren 1989).

Under Castillo Armas, the country was soon reopened to a large number of foreign clergy of all nationalities and political stripes in a decentralization effort that led to more Roman Catholic priests and sisters in the countryside (Warren 1989: 92–93). In order to make Scripture and Catholic ideology more palatable to the rural population, Catholic missionaries and catechists reoriented their teachings toward economic and political issues (Fischer 2001: 91). David Stoll described one of the new Catholic orders, the Missionaries of the Sacred Heart, which, like other postcoup Catholic groups, was charged in 1955 with defending Guatemalans against both communism and the evangelical missions (1988: 102). However, their shock at the treatment of indigenous laborers by their ladino bosses led them to launch development projects in the department of El Quiché and to help to create new village committees.

THE INDIAN PROBLEM

Historians have documented how neither of the revolutionary governments nor Castillo Armas particularly focused on the "Indian problem," the ideology that Guatemala's indigenous majority posed a problem for the nation. In contrast, ethnographers have shown how and whether response to the revolutionary governments' programs did have impacts particular to distinct ethnic groups.

Richard Adams compares the political campaigns between Federico Ponce Vaides (who took power after Ubico's resignation) and Arévalo, both informed by liberal philosophy. Each advanced different ideas in their platforms for the future of Guatemalan Mayas (1990: 154). While Ponce believed that Indians were a separate population who should be targeted for popular support to bolster ladino interests, Arévalo adopted an *indigenista* philosophy that promoted education and health initiatives in order to enculturate Mayas and incorporate them into one singular nation (see also Green 1999: 26–27). The debate came to a head at the 1945 constitutional convention, where the Indian Statute was considered but later rejected. It would have provided specific articles protecting Indian individual and communal lands, as well as promoting cooperatives and intensive training in Spanish (Adams

1990: 155–156). Aside from creating the Instituto Indigenista Nacional (IIN), Arévalo's administration did not set indigenous peoples or other ethnicities as policy priorities or targets of their actions.

While no major reforms or policies of the Arbenz period specifically targeted the ethnicity of indigenous citizens of Guatemala, there were openings, possibilities, and rights granted to them, albeit as campesinos rather than Indians. Shelton Davis notes that the government of Arbenz "attacked the agrarian roots of racial and cultural discrimination in Guatemala" (1988: 14; see also Montejo 2005: 96). However, Carol Smith believes that one of the biggest factors contributing to Arbenz's inability to resist opposition, and later a "weakly organized counterinsurgency force," was his disinterest and ultimate failure in appealing to indigenous Guatemalans as Indians rather than campesinos (1990: 264).

Although many of the changes enacted by the Arévalo and Arbenz administrations arguably had a positive impact on the indigenous populations of Guatemala, policies specifically directed at the Mayas were contentious and often excluded the issue of ethnicity (Nelson 1999: 88–89, 2009: 260; Adams 1990: 154–155). Richard Adams argues that the labor unions, campesino leagues, and political parties did *not* form along ethnic lines and points out that the Castillo Armas regime did not specifically target Indians after the coup—both ladino and indigenous campesinos were affected (1990: 156–157). Likewise, Robert Carmack explains that in Momostenango those jailed after the coup were imprisoned as "pro-Communists," not as Indian troublemakers (1995: 223–224).

SOCIOLOGICAL AWAKENINGS AND ELECTORAL OPENINGS

The ethnographic literature richly demonstrates how Mayas and rural poor were actively engaged with the state during and after the revolutionary period, mostly as new initiatives related to their lived experiences at the community level. Shortly after the coup, Richard Adams headed a project to study dissidents and others jailed by the Castillo Armas government in which he found that the political teachings and activities of the revolutionary period "had left little ideological imprint," but that "an important sociological awakening" had taken place (1988: 290). He later found that this "awakening . . . [was] not squelched by subsequent repressions, but . . . [provided] the groundwork for the revolutionary era that is with us today" (1990: 158).

The democratic openings before the coup set the stage for both ladino and indigenous leaders to challenge incumbents in municipal elections and later allow for a more active indigenous voice in municipal government. Arévalo encouraged juridical reform that separated religious and civil offices within communities (undercutting the *cofradía* system), and Arbenz would later restructure election procedures throughout the country in order to encourage the formation of new political parties (Annis 1987: 43; Adams 1957). Within indigenous communities, this led to a curtailing of ladino power allowing for an increase in Maya political influence. Carmack describes how after the introduction of the two major revolutionary parties in Momostenango, FPL (Frente Popular Libertador) and PAR (Partido de Acción Revolucionaria), Indians dominated local politics by taking advantage of a more democratic electoral process (1995: 226). In many communities, Maya mayors were elected who "defined electoral politics in accordance with their own interests" (C. Smith 1990: 263; cf. T. Smith 2009; Montejo 2005: 114–115; Moors 1988: 70–71; Stoll 1993: 42–43; Adams 1990: 155). Even after Castillo Armas, "electoral politics continued to secularize the countryside" (Annis 1987: 62).

Under Arbenz's presidency, the revolutionary period substantially changed the political consciousness of younger indigenous youth, who found new leadership alternatives to the old vanguard of traditionalists and loyalty to the cargo system (Warren 1989: 12, citing Adams 1957; Watanabe 1992, 1990: 192). Some of Arbenz's reforms encouraged Guatemala's indigenous people to organize and pursue higher education (Montejo 2005: 70). Montejo credits these extracommunal political experiences as underwriting future relationships between indigenous youth (as well as lower-class ladinos) and the more "radical" movements of the 1970s and 1980s, including the Committee for Peasant Unity (Montejo 2005: 88).

The main revolutionary ideas that were adopted by locals had more to do with public works, material progress, and who would control municipal offices and religious rituals, than grand ideas of revolution or reform (Carmack 1995: 229). After the coup, Castillo Armas established new initiatives that both acknowledged the rural interests in the social reforms of 1944–54 and stemmed dissent against the counterrevolution: agricultural cooperatives, land colonization programs, and collaborative development projects with the Roman Catholic Church and U.S. Peace Corps (Warren 1989: 13; Montejo 2005: 114–115).

THE ELEPHANT IN THE ROOM:
PRIMACY OF THE AGRARIAN REFORM

While many scholars usually focus upon the conclusion that Arbenz sealed his fate by alienating what little internal support he had when he launched his ambitious agrarian reform (not to mention giving the Dulles brothers a reason to involve the United States), ethnographers have documented the impact of land reform at the community level before the coup. The agrarian crisis in Guatemala was accelerated by a growing population not supported by highly unequal land distribution, and the increase of seasonal migration led to higher levels of migrant labor and debt peonage (Davis 1988: 14–15).

In a 1975 review of five ethnographies addressing Guatemalan communities directly before and after the 1954 coup, Robert Wasserstrom showed that the authors' own data demonstrate stratification in all five communities, regardless of the communities' (quite contrasting) ethnic composition. In each community, the bulk of arable lands were concentrated in the hands of a few before and after 1944–54. Nevertheless, Wasserstrom found that the anthropologists paid scant attention to these dynamics. A Mexicanist, he wondered if his senior Guatemalanist colleagues had been "seduced by the exoticism of Indian life . . . rather than discovering the forces which induced poverty and inequality among both Indians and Ladinos" (1975: 470–475).

According to Warren, the revolutionary governments had little impact on San Andrés Semetebaj until the establishment of a local agrarian reform committee in 1952, which led to ethnic tensions. She recounts oral histories of indigenous Catholics describing a growing sentiment that Ubico's administration, through universalistic education and taxation, fostered unity across ethnic lines. However, the Arbenz period is remembered as one of "increased antagonism between Indian laborers and ladino *patrones*" (Warren 1989: 152). In local accounts, landholders were afraid of losing their lands and Indian laborers were fearful that any changes were tenuous at best. The coup was well received by both ladinos and Indians alike, and Castillo Armas was remembered as calming these community divisions, most notably in his extending an olive branch to those who had participated in the agrarian reform committees.

In paraphrasing a ladino who moved to Momostenango in the 1940s, Robert Carmack reports that agrarian reform was of little consequence given that no Momostecan received land on the coast and no labor unions were organized (1995: 223–224, 229–230). In northern Quiché, the agrarian reform had only started to affect local communities by the time of the coup. While there were some arrests after the coup, it appears that the Ixil communities were spared the bloodshed of other regions (Stoll 1993: 42–43).

Most scholars today would agree that Arbenz's ambitious plan was in no way a sign that communists were running amok in his administration. Drawing upon the work of historian Jim Handy, anthropologist Edward Fischer points out that Arbenz was targeting feudalism with the agrarian reform, a reform necessary to develop a more robust capitalist agricultural economy as the foundation for his economic program (2001: 74–75, 86–87, citing Handy 1984: 103; 1990: 168). The great irony is that "the revolutionary governments of 1945 to 1954, commonly viewed in the United States and Guatemala as socialist or Communist (a perception that ultimately led to their downfall), subscribed to [the] ideas of capitalist economic growth" (Fischer 1996: 53).

Ethnographic Reflections on the Legacy of the Coup

The contributors for this volume, all anthropologists or ethnographically trained researchers, worked in Guatemala between 1944 and 1954, during the coup itself, the 1950s, 1960s, 1970s, and 1980s amid acute armed conflict and genocidal counterinsurgency, and during the "long" decade of the 1990s peace process.

One of the unforeseen outcomes of the conference was that we have a great deal to say beyond the coup of 1954 and the impact it had on U.S.–Latin American relations. The work here is enriched by the role that anthropology plays in the retelling of history and the introduction of new historiographies and methods by which we capture past events in our writings. These essays move away from the view of history as a series of events and toward history as what happens "between" events. In fact, none of the contributors draw specifically on the new information made available by the declassification of the U.S. government documents concerning "PBSUCCESS," that is, Guatemala 1954. The writers untangle the ongoing consequences of 1954, such as the abrupt change in state policies, the disrupting of complex pre-1954 multirooted Guatemalan-U.S. relations, the impact of those set of years on social structure, popular memory, indigenous identity formation, and state-community political relationships.

The U.S. government's complicity in the violence that Guatemalans have endured, however, has deeply affected the anthropology of any U.S.-based researcher. Many of our essays note the shift from naïveté to activist research agendas, from community-based studies to world systems, dependency, and national frameworks of analysis, as well as the polarization of research choices and agendas. All of the contributors attempt to present what the processes linked to Guatemala 1954 looked like from Guatemala, rather than from the United States. All are carefully nonpresentist, particularly when the material is from people no longer able to defend themselves. In short, all of the authors have moved away from the trope of the 1954 U.S.-CIA coup and on to Guatemala and Guatemalans before, during, and after the coup. In doing so, the essays in no way diminish the fact of an event that can only be described as a watershed; all of the essays lead back to a deeper understanding of the 1954 Guatemalan coup.

In her chapter, Abigail Adams discusses some of the issues raised about national integration during and after the coup by providing an in-depth account of Antonio Goubaud Carrera, a prominent Guatemalan anthropologist. Her account counters historically prevalent fears that government institutions addressing "the Indian problem" in Guatemala might be exclusionary and divisive. In fact, her critical summary of his work shows that his goal as the first director of the IIN was an inclusive program geared toward a homogenous Guatemalan national identity that favored citizenship as opposed to assimilation. This is an important contribution for understanding the origins of the Guatemalan intelligentsia's views of the country's indigenous population and defends against traditional critiques of indigenismo in Latin America.

June Nash's honest and personal account of her life before, during, and after the coup raises important issues about how anthropologists engage with local communities and their members. She provides a first-person account of life in Guatemala around the 1954 coup and mirrors it with updates from return trips in 2002 and 2005. She discusses a move (which defines most of anthropological work in post-1954 Guatemala) from naive fieldwork to activism and solidarity. It also highlights a shift from indirect complicity to a politicized interest in countering U.S. policy in the twentieth century, which some may argue lies at the heart of current applications for engaged anthropology.

David Carey Jr.'s contribution could be interpreted as a larger critique and useful safeguard against viewing the 1954 coup as a watershed event in Guatemalan history, at least from an indigenous perspective. His emphasis on Maya perspectives on the coup from Mayan speakers in the Kaqchikel region calls into question the emphasis that non-Guatemalan intellectuals (namely, anthropologists) place upon the coup. He effectively argues that the Maya community members whom he interviewed did not think much of the revolution of 1944 or the 1954 coup largely due to a disinterest in the state, which historically has been viewed as backing local ladino interests. The reforms and promises that the Arévalo and Arbenz administrations made to the rural and Maya communities were seen as secondary to the unstable and dangerous fragility of democracy. Instead, his chapter shows a Maya preference for strongman caudillo politics because, at the very least, Mayas knew who they were dealing with, most especially at the local level.

He drives home the central point that our understandings and analyses of Guatemalan history must take into account an indigenous perspective, and he shows the importance of unofficial and oral histories.

Christa Little-Siebold offers a glimpse into the impact of peasant leagues on identity politics in eastern Guatemala. Her chapter illustrates the oft-ignored or overlooked ways in which ladinos and indigenous peasants have formed alliances or shared a common identity through the uniting rubric of land and campesino status. She shows how government and outsider labeling was either rejected or failed to map onto local constructions of identity. Her research highlights the complexities of ethnicity, and her discussion of inter-ethnic alliances, many times out of convenience, challenges us to reexamine how our own view of the coup's impact and politicization (or lack thereof) may hinder our realization of what was taking place and has continued to take place under the radar of the national. The research provided in her chapter illustrates the changing nature of what it means to be campesino and how that has played into the recollection or forgetting of the coup, given the ways in which the events of 1954 were filtered through local understandings and conflicts.

In her survey of the history of the official nonrecognition of Mayan languages in Guatemala, Judith Maxwell gives a specific understanding of the relationship between Maya intellectuals and the state in postcoup Guatemala. She details the initiation of various government programs, some with failure and some with success, aimed at increasing educational opportunities for Maya citizens. Throughout its efforts, first in Spanish and later in the Mayan languages, the government has since about 1960 offered an alternative path toward national integration (again, not assimilation) for Mayan speakers. In fact, we could argue that one of the strongest bases for an urban-based Maya movement in the latter half of the twentieth century came in the form of language standardization and efforts to build effective bilingual education programs in Guatemala. This however, as Maxwell shows, had its roots in the revolutionary and epi-coup periods.

Richard Adams's historical chapter highlights the dynamics of the revolutionary period (1944–54) within rural Guatemala. He shows an increasing emergence of Indians on the national scene far before the recently emphasized Pan-Maya movement of the 1980s and 1990s. He argues that revolutionary reforms opened spaces for Indians to recover political power on the local level, which has had larger implications for national incorporation and laying the groundwork for the work of Maya nationalists in the late twentieth century. In fact, he supports a view that the successes of Pan-Maya activism in the urban sector post–Peace Accords were "delayed" in the rural communities, much in part due to a historical dismissal of ethnicity and difference by both anthropology and the Guatemalan state.

Finally, we are proud to include as an epilogue the keynote address delivered by then–Secretary of Peace Victor Montejo at the 2005 University of Illinois conference, "From a Springtime of Democracy to a Winter of Cold War: The 1954 Guatemalan Coup and Its Lasting Impact on U.S./Latin American Relations."[1] Dr. Montejo had just overseen the initial process of developing, negotiating, and delivering the long-promised compensation to victims of the violence. His words at the close of the conference, and fifty years after the opening year of post-1954 Guatemala, revealed how terrible the violence against supporters of the revolution had been and spoke to the complexities faced by members of a post-*violencia* society attempting civil reconstruction. Dr. Montejo, Jakaltek Maya, Guatemalan, former small-town public schoolteacher and now an internationally renowned writer and anthropologist, serves as a model for how anthropologists can respond to their multiple locations among the people they study with a repertoire of inquiry, method, analysis, and publication.

Note

1. In both an ironic and perhaps strategic move, then-President Oscar Berger Perdomo took the opportunity of Dr. Montejo's absence to fire and publicly denounce him in the Guatemalan press on the day of his keynote address. Montejo had already planned to resign upon his return because of debilitating cuts to his office's budget and over concerns that he might have been chosen as a token Maya member in Berger's cabinet (Nash 2007: 120).

Works Cited

Adams, Richard N., ed.
  1957   Political Changes in Rural Guatemalan Communities: A Symposium. Middle American Research Institute, pub. 4. New Orleans: Tulane University.
Adams, Richard N.
  1988   Conclusions: What Can We Know about the Harvest of Violence? *In* Harvest of Violence. Robert M. Carmack, ed. Pp. 274–292.
  1990   Ethnic Images and Strategies in 1944. *In* Guatemalan Indians and the State, 1540–1988. Carol A. Smith, ed. Pp. 141–162. Austin: University of Texas Press.
Annis, Sheldon
  1987   God and Production in a Guatemalan Town. Austin: University of Texas Press.

Aybar de Soto, José
1978   Dependency and Intervention: The Case of Guatemala 1954. Boulder, Colo.: Westview Press.

Carmack, Robert M., ed.
1988   Harvest of Violence: The Maya Indians and the Guatemalan Crisis. Norman: University of Oklahoma Press.

Carmack, Robert M.
1995   Rebels of Highland Guatemala: The Quiché-Mayas of Momostenango. Norman: University of Oklahoma Press.

Davis, Shelton H.
1988   Introduction: Sowing the Seeds of Violence. In Harvest of Violence. Robert M. Carmack, ed. Pp. 3–38.

Fischer, Edward F.
1996   Induced Culture Change as a Strategy for Socioeconomic Development: The Pan-Maya Movement of Guatemala. In Maya Cultural Activism. Edward F. Fischer and R. McKenna Brown, eds. Pp. 51–73. Austin: University of Texas Press.
2001   Cultural Logics and Global Economies: Maya Identity in Thought and Practice. Austin: University of Texas Press.

Gleijeses, Piero
1991   Shattered Hope: The Guatemalan Revolution and the United States 1944–1954. Princeton, N.J.: Princeton University Press.

Grandin, Greg
2000   The Blood of Guatemala: A History of Race and Nation. Durham, N.C.: Duke University Press.
2004   The Last Colonial Massacre: Latin America in the Cold War. Chicago: University of Chicago Press.

Green, Linda
1999   Fear as a Way of Life: Mayan Widows in Rural Guatemala. New York: Columbia University Press.

Handy, Jim
1984   Gift of the Devil: A History of Guatemala. Boston: South End Press.
1988   National Policy, Agrarian Reform, and the Corporate Community during the Guatemalan Revolution, 1944–54. Comparative Studies in Society and History 30 (October): 698–724.
1990   The Corporate Community, Campesino Organizations, and Agrarian Reform: 1950–1954. In Guatemalan Indians and the State: 1540–1988. Carol A. Smith, ed. Pp. 163–182. Austin: University of Texas Press.
1994   Revolution in the Countryside: Rural Conflict and Agrarian Reform in Guatemala, 1944–1954. Chapel Hill: University of North Carolina Press.

Immerman, Richard H.
1982   The CIA in Guatemala. Austin: University of Texas Press.

Manz, Beatriz
　2004　Paradise in Ashes: A Guatemalan Journey of Courage, Terror and Hope. Berkeley: University of California Press.
Montejo, Victor D.
　1999　Voices from Exile: Violence and Survival in Modern Maya History. Norman: University of Oklahoma Press.
　2005　Maya Intellectual Renaissance. Austin: University of Texas Press.
Moors, Marilyn M.
　1988　Indian Labor and the Guatemalan Crisis. *In* Central America: Historical Perspectives on the Contemporary Crises. R. C. Woodward Jr., ed. Pp. 67–84. New York: Greenwood Press.
　2005　Maya Intellectual Renaissance. Austin: University of Texas Press.
Nash, June C.
　2007　Practicing Ethnography in a Globalizing World: An Anthropological Odyssey. Lanham, Md.: AltaMira Press.
Nelson, Diane M.
　1999　A Finger in the Wound: Body Politics in Quincentennial Guatemala. Berkeley: University of California Press.
　2009　Reckoning: The Ends of War in Guatemala. Durham, N.C.: Duke University Press.
Schlesinger, Stephen, and Stephen Kinzer
　1982　Bitter Fruit: The Story of the American Coup in Guatemala. New York: Doubleday and Anchor Books.
Sinclair, Minor, ed.
　1995　The New Politics of Survival: Grassroots Movements in Central America. New York: Monthly Review Press.
Smith, Carol A.
　1990　Conclusion: History and Revolution in Guatemala. *In* Guatemalan Indians and the State, 1540–1988. Carol A. Smith, ed. Pp. 258–286. Austin: University of Texas Press.
Smith, Timothy J.
　2009　Democracy Is Dissent: Political Confrontations and Indigenous Mobilization in Sololá. *In* Mayas in Postwar Guatemala: Harvest of Violence Revisited. Walter E. Little and Timothy J. Smith, eds. Pp. 16–29. Tuscaloosa: University of Alabama Press.
Stoll, David
　1988　Evangelicals, Guerrillas, and the Army: The Ixil Triangle Under Ríos Montt. *In* Harvest of Violence. Robert M. Carmack, ed. Pp. 90–118.
　1993　Between Two Armies in the Ixil Towns of Guatemala. New York: Columbia University Press.
Warren, Kay B.
　1989[1978]　Symbolism of Subordination: Indian Identity in a Guatemalan Town. Austin: University of Texas Press.

Wasserstrom, Robert

1975   Revolution in Guatemala: Peasants and Politics under the Arbenz Govern-
        ment. *In* Comparative Studies in Society and History 17:443–78.

Watanabe, John M.

1990   Enduring Yet Ineffable Community in the Western Periphery of Guatemala.
        In Guatemalan Indians and the State, 1540–1988. Carol A. Smith, ed. Pp.
        183–204. Austin: University of Texas Press.

1992   Maya Saints and Souls in a Changing World. Austin: University of Texas
        Press.

Wilkinson, Daniel

2002   Silence on the Mountain: Stories of Terror, Betrayal, and Forgetting in
        Guatemala. New York: Houghton Mifflin.

1

Antonio Goubaud Carrera

Between the Contradictions of the
Generación de 1920 and U.S. Anthropology

ABIGAIL E. ADAMS

In the spirit of this volume's work to recontextualize the events and people from the coup, I take up the life and writings of Antonio Goubaud Carrera, first director of Guatemala's Instituto Indigenista Nacional (IIN). Goubaud is a pivotal figure in the charged relations among Guatemalan indigenists, nationalists, and U.S. anthropologists. Goubaud was dubbed Guatemala's "first anthropologist." A dedicated autodidact, he also pursued formal education at Harvard and his master's degree at the University of Chicago; he was the first professor of anthropology at Guatemala's Universidad de San Carlos. He was also a progressive nationalist. Goubaud was a member of Guatemala's "white" elite, of the Generación de 1920, the 1944 October Revolution, and later, Arévalo's Guatemalan ambassador to the United States.

When the 1954 coup d'état sponsored by the U.S. Central Intelligence Agency (CIA) destroyed Guatemala's new democracy, it also destroyed the IIN, the institution Goubaud had built from scratch. In the contortions of the ensuing cold war years, Goubaud's reputation, contributions, and hopes for his nation and Maya majority were destroyed as well. The 1954 coup impoverished and flattened a rich set of intellectual and institutional relationships that were developing between the United States and Guatemala.

Recent publications reflect the damage done throughout the postcoup years. Several studies state that Goubaud and the IIN promoted cultural assimilation of Guatemala's Maya communities. For example, one cites "an especially straightforward policy statement from a 1956 IIN document: 'The Indian with more buying power and with national culture will be a better producer and consumer and a more active citizen. To achieve this we must adapt him scientifically through our acculturation program'" (Fischer 2001: 69–70, citing Nelson 1999: 90).

The quotation above lacks a historical treatment of the IIN document; it was published two years after the coup ended the October Revolution. The coup leaders, who were responsible for the mass murder of peasants, indigenous and nonindigenous alike, also murdered those involved with the IIN (Forster 2001; Grandin 2004; Handy 1994). They imprisoned Goubaud's successor at the IIN, Joaquín Noval, who registered as a member of the Partido Guatemalteco de Trabajo, Guatemala's communist party, after the coup (R. N. Adams 2000). Following the coup, any IIN influence within the state bureaucracy plummeted. By the late 1960s, the institution consisted of a few paid officials who had no working funds (Marroquín 1972). The IIN was eliminated in the mid-1980s.[1]

The IIN, like the seven-year-old CIA that destroyed it, was an institution that emerged to address the problems of the post–World War II era. Goubaud inaugurated the IIN during September 1945, the month that peace was established in the Pacific theater of World War II, following the atomic bombing of Japan. Goubaud explicitly placed the IIN's inauguration in the context of postwar world events, stating: "I want to say that compared to international anarchy, Guatemala's problem with ethnic diversity might seem small. But for us, it is our fundamental problem . . . among all of the ethnic groups of Guatemala's nationality, indigenous as well as non-indigenous, there exists a marked desire for a greater mutual understanding. . . . We should say that this desire and our response is the mechanism by which a true nationality will be formed, one in which a large measure of understandings are common, current and shared by all of the inhabitants of the nation" (Goubaud Carrera 1964: 24).

Goubaud's inauguration speech is the text largely cited in references to the IIN. Two lines are commonly pulled from this speech: one in which Goubaud describes *indigenismo* as a symptom of social discomfort, and another in which he refers to a "homogeneous nationality."[2] Some scholars have interpreted the term he used for social discomfort, "malestar social," to imply that Goubaud considered indigenous peoples as an organic "disease" and proposed the erasure of indigenous culture.[3]

Another scholar combined the selected lines from the inauguration speech with Goubaud's status as a Guatemalan elite, and with his associations with U.S. anthropologists, particularly Robert Redfield and Solomon Tax. He concluded that Goubaud imprinted Guatemalan anthropology with an "applied" focus aimed to acculturate Indians and create subjects of the state, thereby laying the institutional and ideological foundations for the counterinsurgent state's 1980s genocide (Gonzalez Ponciano 1997).

Goubaud's full speech, however, makes it clear that he was not proposing a eugenics solution for the "Indian problem." Instead, Goubaud laid out a full program for the IIN. He was committed to cultural relativism and referred to Guatemala's "two cultures," indigenous and nonindigenous, as valid. While talking about "culturas disímiles," he stated clearly that these were not distinct cultures, that Mayas and non-Mayas shared quite a bit with each other. One trait that members of either culture shared was a lack of national identity as Guatemalan citizens. In other words, *no one* was participating in a national culture. The speech is also remarkably free of romantic glorification of the Mayas, and is instead directly focused on areas of concern for all Guatemalans.

In the next four years, from 1945 through 1949, Goubaud accomplished all and more of what he set out in his inaugural speech. In this chapter, I describe his considerable achievements. I also explore the significant and heterodox intellectual currents informing Goubaud, the IIN, and the North American and Guatemalan anthropological encounter.[4] Among these currents were diverse "indigenist" positions held by Guatemala's famous Generación de 1920 and intellectual predecessors. For example, many different positions are at stake in the term that Goubaud used in his 1945 inaugural speech, "national homogeneity." By the mid-twentieth century, other Latin American countries with indigenous majorities were promoting various forms of *mestizaje* in their nationalist imaginaries, but elite Guatemalans continued promoting "homogeneous nationality" to address what they saw as the "Indian problem." The Indian problem is the thesis that indigenous peoples would hold back national development and entrance into Euro-centered modernity.

The Guatemalan elite indigenist discourses were deeply influenced, in turn, by the ethnologies already established in Guatemala by North Americans and Europeans, particularly Germans whose writings reflected an influential movement based on the emerging German notion of culture and science of ethnology. By the 1940s, Guatemala's indigenist intellectual production became intertwined with a shift in theoretical hegemony in U.S. anthropology as well, away from the German-dominated ethnology, from historical to synchronic approaches, from spirituality, culture, and personality to social change and comparative economics.

Goubaud, who spoke and wrote unaccented English, French, and German as well as Spanish, was well-read in all these schools (Gillin 1952b: 71–73). Later he would study Mayan languages, particularly Kaqchikel. Goubaud is firmly placed among those "organic intellectuals" identified by Marta Elena

Casaús Arzú, who emerged from Guatemala's elite families and who coalesced thinking that both served and challenged elite interests.[5]

Goubaud's orientation to the United States is marked throughout his biography as well and is intimately connected to his indigenist vocation. He graduated from a U.S. high school, studied a semester at Harvard, and then worked in Guatemala for U.S. expatriate Alfred Clark, of Clark Tours, through whom he met University of Chicago anthropologists Solomon Tax and Robert Redfield. Later, while studying at the University of Chicago, he met the U.S. fine arts student Frances Westbrook, who would become his wife. The couple was working in Guatemala with Tax and the Carnegie Institution when Goubaud was called to help found Guatemala's IIN.

Goubaud left the IIN directorship in 1949 to serve as Guatemala's ambassador to the United States at the request of President Juan José Arévalo. His appointment ended tragically March 8, 1951, when Goubaud was found dead in his room in Guatemala City after meetings with Arévalo. A few days later, Jacobo Arbenz Guzmán assumed the presidency of Guatemala. The causes of Goubaud's death remain unclear, although the event has been framed by at least two of his biographers as an assassination (Mendoza 1994: 26–36; Vela 1956).

After reviewing Goubaud's relationships, writings, and politico-intellectual networks, I conclude that Goubaud was a complex, evolving thinker and a highly experienced fieldworker who did not promote racialist views of Maya peoples. As anthropologist Carol Smith has pointed out, Guatemala's governors have had relatively little knowledge of life in indigenous communities (1990: 18). Goubaud was a marked exception, then, to this rule, and he diligently and publicly opposed Guatemalans searching for sweeping racialist solutions to the "Indian problem."

Antonio Goubaud Carrera, 1902–1951

My interest in Goubaud began as a coincidence: Goubaud worked in both the isolated Oriente township of Jocotán, with Ch'orti' Mayas, and in San Juan Chamelco, Alta Verapaz, where I worked as well. In his field notes, I found a like-minded colleague who was appalled by the poverty of Jocotán and charmed by the green beauty and seemingly progressive racial relations of the Verapaz.[6] Goubaud later proved to be an invaluable resource in my research of a spirit possession cult in rural San Juan Chamelco, a cult that reemerged during Guatemala's quincentenary year, 1992 (A. E. Adams 2009, 2001, 1999, 1996). The cult is utterly undocumented in the considerable ethnography on

Q'eqchi' Mayan speakers and the Verapaz, with one exception: Goubaud's 1944 field notes, in which he describes cultivating a relationship with an ancestor of today's spirit mediums (A. E. Adams 2008; see also A. E. Adams 1999).

Although I first scoured his notes for facts about my dissertation field site, and later, my new work with Maya spirit mediums, my interest in Goubaud has continued through his connections with the Generación de 1920 and Arévalo's presidency.[7] I have had the pleasure of working with Goubaud's daughters, resulting in an exchange of materials concerning their father that has proved mutually informative.

Goubaud was born August 17, 1902, a year after David Vela, the Generación de 1920 member to whom he was closest. His birthright included membership in those elite family networks identified by Marta Elena Casaús Arzú. On two sides of his family, his paternal grandmother, Jesús Oyarzabal y Mendia, and his mother, Maria Carrera Wyld, were members of the original Basque elites of Guatemala. His paternal grandfather, Émile Goubaud, provided the connection to northern European nineteenth-century immigrants, who brought capital and connections and quickly gained placement in the Guatemalan elite's family networks. Grand-père Émile Goubaud immigrated to Guatemala in 1853 from the French island of Ré, off the Breton coast, and represented a French publishing house. He founded the first bookstore in Central America and became one of Guatemala's first coffee exporters. He also founded a large family with his Basque-descent bride, Jesús Oyarzabal y Mendia, with whom he had eleven children (Gillin 1952b; Vela 1956).[8]

One of their children, Goubaud's father, Alberto Goubaud, was a well-to-do coffee planter and exporter. He and his wife, Maria Carrera, had four children. Alberto died suddenly during a visit in Paris when the children were quite young. Antonio's mother became incapacitated and unable to care for her children, who were placed with relatives. Antonio was sent to the United States at the age of fifteen to continue his education, an arrangement facilitated by coffee exporter John Wright of San Francisco.[9]

Because of his family's situation, the course of Goubaud's education and upbringing differs from that of more well-known members of the Generación de 1920 cast. Unlike them, Goubaud did not attend the Instituto Nacional Central para Varones, join the Huelga de Dolores and other oppositions to Estrada Cabrera, or matriculate at the Universidad de San Carlos. He received his elementary schooling in private German academies in Guatemala, his secondary education at the Colegio Alemán of Guatemala City. In 1916, he was sent to California, where he completed high school at the Christian Brothers of La Salle's St. Mary's College in the Bay area.

St. Mary's College then, as it is now, was dedicated to the liberal arts.[10] The college has always matriculated Latin American students and was active in Latin American Catholic circles.[11] Goubaud was enrolled in the college's high school program from 1917 through 1921.[12] He followed the standard four-year high school curriculum, with foreign language, history, vocal expression, science (chemistry, biology, physics), math, civics, music, drawing, and religion. He also appears as a featured solo or duet violinist on several special programs, such as the college graduation and awards ceremonies.[13]

College archives do not reveal that Goubaud belonged to any special club dedicated to indigenous issues, but John Gillin records that "[Goubaud's] interest in Indians had been aroused while in the United States, and he set himself to reading and acquiring all the books on this subject he could obtain." Goubaud arrived in California's Bay area at a time of heightened interest in American Indians: that year its most famous indigenous resident, Ishi, died. Ishi, "the last wild Indian," had been living in the University of California's Museum of Anthropology in Golden Gate Park, where he received many visitors and media coverage in life and, later, in death (Gillin 1952b).[14]

When Goubaud returned to Guatemala in 1921, he worked for a British import-export business (Gillin 1952b; Rubinstein 2002; Vela 1956). Two years later the influential Sociedad de Geografía e Historia (SGH) was organized. The SGH was modeled on "the [learned societies] that exist in almost all the nations of Latin America, in the United States and many countries of Europe."[15] As Carol Hendrickson notes, given the place in government and civil life of many of the SGH's first members, "many of the SGH's goals dovetailed with government projects or with projects that the members thought the government should assume" (1997). Its first vice president, Virgilio Rodríguez Beteta, spoke of Guatemala's geographical, material, and intellectual isolation, and of the need to catch up with the "march of civilization measured by Hertzian waves and heavy with the iron of subways" (Rodríguez Betata 1924, cited in Hendrickson 1997).

Goubaud participated regularly in SGH meetings and in the public intellectual activities of its members. He was elected a member in 1935, presenting his induction essay on the Maya calendar celebration, "El 'Guajxaquip Bats.'" He translated his induction essay into English and worked on translating (Spanish to English, English to Spanish, German to Spanish) other scholars' works. He translated into Spanish Otto Stoll's classic work, *Zur Ethnographie der Republik Guatemala* (1884). He had previously begun, with Herbert Sapper, the translation into Spanish of Leonhard Schultze Jena's (1933) *I—Leben, Glaube und Sprache der Quiché von Guatemala*. With Robert Smith, he also translated from Spanish to English the SGH's argument for Guatemala's right to British Honduras (1938a).

Goubaud undertook study of Kaqchikel Mayan, with the aim of developing a curriculum for the language. In the mid-1930s, he took an introductory anthropology course at Harvard, while on an extended stay in the Boston area. During the course, he met Clyde Kluckhohn and other members of Harvard's distinguished anthropology department (Vela 1956). He joined several U.S. learned societies, including the American Anthropological Association, the American Ethnological Association, and the New York Academy of Sciences, and subscribed to their publications from Guatemala.

He also changed jobs, to further his commitment to anthropology and to support his family. Goubaud left the import-export business in 1934 to work for Alfred Clark's tours. By all reports, he made this move in order to work more closely in the field of his avocation, the study of indigenous cultures (Gillin 1952b; Rubinstein 2002; Vela 1956). He served as a tour guide for European and North American visitors interested in visiting Maya villages, precisely at that moment when Clark was canonizing Chichicastenango and the towns of Lake Atitlán as Guatemala's tourist experience.

In 1934 Clark introduced Goubaud to University of Chicago anthropologist Solomon Tax and his wife, Gertrude.[16] Tax, two years younger than Goubaud, warmed to him quickly, and wrote at length about the Guatemalan amateur ethnologist in a letter to his director, Robert Redfield. Redfield responded with initial enthusiasm, offering to employ Goubaud in the future, but cautioning Tax not to disclose this offer to Goubaud. For the next five years, Goubaud kept in contact with the two anthropologists. He visited Chichicastenango, where Tax was struggling with fieldwork, and gathered material for his 1935 SGH essay. Goubaud did not work for Redfield or Tax before he began studies in 1939 at the University of Chicago. At Chicago he completed some undergraduate prerequisites and entered graduate school for anthropology. In 1942 he undertook fieldwork on nutrition in Spanish American communities in Taos and Cundiyo, New Mexico.[17]

That year he married Frances Westbrook of Wheaton, Illinois, a fellow University of Chicago student and artist. David Vela stood as Goubaud's witness; he was in the United States as a guest of the U.S. State Department and of Bureau of Indian Affairs Director John Collier. Vela took the opportunity to discuss with Goubaud the idea of a Guatemalan indigenist institute, inspired by the Primer Congreso Indigenista Interamericano, which Vela attended in 1940 in Pátzcuaro, Mexico (Vela 1956).

Goubaud received his master's degree in anthropology from the University of Chicago in 1943, presenting his thesis, "Food Patterns and Nutrition in Two Spanish-American Communities." He returned to Guatemala to work for the Carnegie Institution of Washington. For two years, he conducted comparative research on the nutritional practices of Indians and ladinos in three municipios (see Goubaud 1946c, 1948, 1949c, and 1949e).[18]

In the midst of this research, in 1944, Jorge Ubico y Castañeda was overthrown. Goubaud was called back to Guatemala City to establish the long-delayed Instituto Indigenista Nacional, which Ubico had thwarted during his fourteen years in power. Goubaud was named the IIN's first director and went on to found both the Museo Nacional de Arqueología y Etnología and a new administrative unit of the Guatemalan government, the Instituto de Antropología e Historia. He was also named principal professor of anthropology at the Universidad de San Carlos, in addition to creating and editing the *Boletín del IIN*, which later was published as *Guatemala Indígena*. He drew up a program for the IIN that combined academic research with applied projects. With the U.S. anthropologist Benjamin Paul, he wrote a "Guia para las investigaciones de campo" for scholars preparing monographs in different municipios.[19] Under Goubaud's stewardship, the IIN also prepared pamphlets in Mayan languages on the laws of Guatemala, with recommendations for communities on how to participate more effectively in the legal system.

Goubaud cut a swath through international circles on indigenous affairs. In 1947 Goubaud traveled to Europe, first to England as a guest of the British Council, and then to Paris as a consultant for the United Nations Educational, Scientific and Cultural Organization (UNESCO). He was Guatemala's delegate to the International Labor Organization (ILO) conference, which met 1949 in Montevideo, Uruguay. That same year, he traveled to the United Nations in New York to serve as a consultant on native problems. In January 1951, he assumed the chair of the first session of the ILO's Committee of Experts on Indigenous Labor, which convened in La Paz, Bolivia. He was a foreign fellow of the American Anthropological Association and a member of the Royal Anthropological Institute of the United Kingdom (Gillin 1952b). Meanwhile, whether in Guatemala or elsewhere, he served as the key contact for many foreign scholars working in Guatemala.[20]

In January 1950, Goubaud took a leave of absence from the IIN in order to serve as ambassador to the United States for President Juan José Arévalo. He took the post with considerable reservations. Arévalo requested personally that Goubaud assume the post, after Guatemala and the United States had severed diplomatic relations and sent home their respective ambassadors, Jorge Garcia Granados and Richard Patterson. Vela observed, "Admirer of that people, knowledgeable of its culture and customs, affiliate with its universities and scientific societies, Goubaud was an ideal link to reconnect and maintain friendly relations" (1956).

As ambassador, Goubaud continued to champion Guatemalan anthropology. Gillin reports that "Goubaud was the first professionally trained anthropologist anywhere to be named ambassador in charge of a permanently established mission" (1952b). He worked closely with the U.S. Institute of Social Anthropology (ISA), and requested that a field anthropologist be sent to Guatemala through the ISA program with the U.S. State Department.[21]

U.S.-Guatemalan relations, however, continued to deteriorate, as did the relation between Arévalo and Goubaud. In 1951 Goubaud was recalled to Guatemala for meetings that he found humiliating and demeaning.[22] After several tense confrontations, Goubaud was found dead in his private rooms, both wrists slashed and a deep cut in the back of his head. His body was received for a wake at the National Palace and buried the following day in Guatemala City's General Cemetery. The mysterious circumstances surrounding Goubaud's death have never been satisfactorily resolved.

He was survived by his wife, Frances, and two daughters, Cristina and Monica. Frances never returned to Guatemala, although Goubaud's anthropology colleagues helped her settle her family in Albuquerque, where she taught art at the Albuquerque Indian School. Monica became an anthropologist and public health specialist.

Goubaud and Guatemala's Debate over "El Indio y la Nación"

Goubaud was an active participant in nationalist intellectual debates concerning the "Indian problem." By the mid-twentieth century, Guatemala was stuck, seemingly incapable of imagining anything other than a white Western nation. While other Latin American nations were appropriating images of their pre-Columbian roots and potential racial fusion, Guatemala's intellectuals were discussing the concept of "homogeneous nationality," which was based on fashionable eugenicist and racialist theories from Europe. Casaús Arzú argues that these intellectual frameworks would reemerge in the 1970s and 1980s to justify the counterinsurgent state's actions, including genocide (2005, 2001). She documents, however, a diversity of intellectual currents and policy considerations, some derived from positivist racialisms, others drawing on antipositivist currents, particularly theosophy and other variants of spiritualism.

One end of the spectrum includes the influential positions of Miguel Án-gel Asturias, Guatemala's Nobel Prize–winning writer, together with like-minded spirits such as Carlos Samayoa Chinchilla, Federico Mora, Jorge García Granados, Eduardo Mayorga, and Epaminondas Quintana. Their theories of racial degeneration were influenced directly by Spencerian positiv-ism and racial theorists such as Gustave Le Bon and Ernest Renan. National projects envisioned by these thinkers promoted eugenics, miscegenation, and immigration of "whiter" North European stocks as "solutions," which excluded indigenous peoples as national subjects. They describe Indians as an inferior or degenerate race, stagnant, wasted, and inbred. Asturias's "So-ciología guatemalteca: el problema social del indio," his 1923 master's thesis presented at the Universidad de San Carlos, is the most debated presentation of this position.

At the other end of the spectrum we find J. Fernando Juarez Muñoz, whose 1931 essay "El indio guatemalteco: ensayo de sociología nacionalista," was pub-lished eight years after Asturias's treatise. Juarez Muñoz, of the Generación de 1898 and a source of inspiration for the Generación de 1920, was president of the SGH when Goubaud joined. Formerly a champion of Spencerian ra-cialism and eugenics, his 1931 essay reflects his conversion to theosophy. His explanation of the "Indian problem" is still racialist, but the "problem" is now the Spanish. Theosophists at that time held that humanity would be saved by the "fifth race," those descended from the "hindus" and from aboriginal Americans (Casaús Arzú 2003, 2001: 20; Campbell 1980; Deves Valdes and Melgar Bao 1999). Juarez Muñoz opposed *mestizaje,* therefore, because any resulting population would suffer from the degenerated gene pool of Span-iards. Furthermore, he opposed acculturation as the nation-building road for Guatemala. He was not a proponent of homogeneous nationality. He proposed that indigenous peoples be incorporated into a "positiva naciona-lidad" through full citizenship, one based on their own culture and identity, access to education, and specific legislation that protected native rights to citizenship and to just work, health care, and education. He adamantly sup-ported indigenous peoples' claim to arable land. Casaús Arzú dubs him "one of the predecessors of Guatemalan indigenist thinking" (2001: 22). Other theosophists were active in the October Revolution, particularly in the first literacy campaigns of Arévalo. Theosophy influenced wider Latin American indigenist circles, foremost among them Mexico, where José Vasconcelos developed the idea of *la raza cósmica.*

Goubaud and David Vela were among the few proponents in Guatemala of the indigenist policies reshaping Mexico. David Vela figures in Goubaud's story, as his life and ambitions intertwine at various moments with Goubaud's—and with U.S. anthropology. The two were born in Guatemala City within a year of each other, and entered indigenist circles, albeit from somewhat different trajectories, together.[23] They were both inducted in the Sociedad de Geografía e Historia in 1935. As already noted, Vela witnessed Goubaud's 1942 wedding to Frances Westbrook in Taos, New Mexico, using the opportunity to discuss the potential for a Guatemalan indigenist institute along the lines of Mexico's. Vela invited Goubaud to join the Grupo Indigenista that eventually founded the IIN and installed him as the IIN's first director. He later urged Goubaud to turn down the U.S. ambassadorship and ultimately wrote one of Goubaud's more influential eulogies, first presented at the Seminario de Integración Social Guatemalteca in 1956 (Vela 1956).[24]

Vela's indigenist work was considerable. Before he became a member of the Sociedad de Geografía e Historia, Vela's writing on archaeology and contemporary indigenous practices presents the Maya race as creators of a magnificent civilization and writers of the *Popol Wuj*.[25] He had met Manuel Gamio—Mexico's anthropologist, student of Franz Boas, and foremost indigenist—who did archaeological work throughout the 1920s in Guatemala's highlands. Gamio advocated a national policy of *mestizaje,* the "national culture of the future." As long as Indians were guided by applied anthropologists, the road would lead to "racial homogeneity, the happy unification of physical types, and the first and most solid basis of nationalism" (1960).

Vela attended the 1940 Pátzcuaro conference on the invitation of Gamio, now at Mexico's Instituto de Antropología e Historia. Vela was not Guatemala's representative, but he headed several commissions at the conference. He returned to Guatemala, and with Ovidio Rodas Corzo, formed the Comisión Indigenista of the Sociedad de Geografía e Historia, later referred to as the Grupo Indigenista. In 1942 he was invited by the U.S. State Department to visit universities and cultural centers; through John Collier, director of the U.S. Bureau of Indian Affairs, he also toured several Southwest Indian reservations of the Apache, Navajo, Papago, and Pueblo peoples. Vela took over *El Imparcial*'s editorship in 1944, which became a forum for indigenist and agrarian policy arguments (and later, the opposition paper to the revolutionary government).

In the October Revolution's constitutional assembly, Vela argued for specific institutions, policies, and laws for Guatemala's indigenous peoples. The revolutionary government did sign the 1940 Pátzcuaro accords, as urged by Vela. But he lost the larger fight: the constitution reflected the opposing position and included no special statuses for indigenous peoples. Vela did succeed in inserting passages that allowed for laws, provisions, and regulations adopted for indigenous groups, "taking into account their needs, conditions, practices, usages and customs" (R. N. Adams 2000; Arriola 1995). These passages were the basis for the creation of the IIN. Vela went on help found the Seminario de Integración Social Guatemalteca in 1956 and served later as its president.

Goubaud himself used the term *homogeneous nationality* in several essays besides his 1945 IIN inaugural address. He opened his 1938 Spanish translation of Otto Stoll's work with a prologue. The prologue's thesis was that Guatemalans needed to read and create their own studies of their country's indigenous majority. The second sentence of the prologue essay stated, "The best way to found homogeneity between the different ethnic sectors is a better understanding of all peoples, rather than an Olympic indifference and ignorance of all [ways of thinking] that differ from an occidental ideology." In the essay, published after his return from a semester at Harvard, he described all Guatemalans as pertaining to an ethnic sector.

In a letter to *El Imparcial*, Goubaud argued again for homogeneous nationality and the pressing need for research. The letter was submitted as part of an early 1937 debate concerning state indigenist policy, sparked by a series of columns by Ramón Aceña Duran, who was reporting from Huehuetenango, and allegedly from experiences with Mam Mayas.[26] Aceña Duran, on January 3, 1937, wrote a column, "El indio incognito," and Goubaud responded that day, in a letter published in parts on January 9 and 11, 1937.

Goubaud, with the diplomacy that served him later, responded to Aceña Duran's highly romantic and ignorant description of a mysterious and closed world of the "more spiritual" Mayas. Goubaud opens and closes his letter with the call for more research of Guatemala's people by Guatemalans themselves, rather than by foreigners. He writes that Guatemalans continued the attitude of the Spanish conquerors by closing their eyes and ignoring the immense ethnic differences between the two cultures, Indian and non-Indian, and by trying to "occidentalize" the Indian. He states clearly that both cultures, indigenous and nonindigenous, were part of Guatemala's ethnic components. He closes the first part of his letter by stating that anthropology had demonstrated that Western man's ways of thinking and living were not the only possible ways. He stated that the complex, coherent Indian mentality "is the equal of ours."

Then, in a passage that today's readers would reject, Goubaud begins a long explanation of how Indian mentality, learned from birth on, was animistic, and therefore Indians confused objects with representations, due to their lack of exposure to a world in which representation was used routinely. He argues that Indians clearly could learn and comprehend, but that whites (*blancos*) could also reflect and analyze.

This letter was written five years into Goubaud's acquaintance with Redfield and Tax, and four months before his departure to the University of Chicago to begin graduate work in anthropology. It reveals the influence of Goubaud's immersion in U.S. anthropology when he argues, in the clear "cultural relativist" sense, that ladinos, Westerners, and indigenous peoples were equal (also see Tax 1941). But his commitment to the Guatemalan debate appeared in the contemporary language of an "Indian problem," and in the vision of a Euro-centered homogeneous nationality.

Goubaud, Germans, Americans, and Indians

Goubaud's acquaintance with U.S. anthropology went beyond the University of Chicago's schools of thought. He was a sophisticated autodidact in the German-inspired schools of anthropology and in German writings on Guatemala. These German traditions arrived in Guatemala with the coffee entrepreneurs and the ethnologists, geographers, technicians, and visitors they brought as well. Goubaud, grandson of a French bookstore owner, and a polyglot himself, entered into Mayanist studies with the distinct advantage of reading German. The German academies in which he completed his elementary and secondary education had been established by the expatriate German coffee and business community in Guatemala City.

German anthropological traditions were rooted in the concept of *Volksgeist*, the "spirit of a people" that would inform the term "culture" contributed by German ethnographers to U.S. anthropology. In German anthropology and among German Indian enthusiasts, a broad intellectual set of movements developed, with one movement quite mystical and in direct opposition to the rationalism of the Enlightenment, another movement with roots in antiquities and the intellectual curiosity stimulated by Charles Étienne Brasseur de Bourbourg's publications, and another dedicated to "science," culture history, and ethnology but also rooted in the concept of cultural essences.[27]

In general, the German scholarship with which Goubaud dealt more seriously after 1921 was on the science and culture history side of interest in Volksgeist, rather than the mystical tradition. These scholars paid attention to methodology and in some cases carried out what we would consider today participant observation. Goubaud's first work was translating German scholars who were interested in the esoteric practices of "traditional" Mayas, such as Leonhard Schultze Jena's work on Chichicastenango Indian practices, which was directly inspired by Brasseur de Bourbourg's work on the "peaceful scientific Maya," and Otto Stoll's linguistic work, which also sought to provide background in order to further understand the creators of the *Popol Wuj*. In 1935 he traveled to Chichicastenango and Momostenango to study the calendar systems, which united science and mysticism or "magic" for his 1935 induction essay, "El 'Guajxaquip Bats,'" into the Sociedad de Geografía e Historia.

In Goubaud's 1945 literature review of Mayanist scholarship, he dedicated the first intellectual stage to German speakers such as Stoll, Seler, Lehman, Schuller, and Termer.[28] The work of Karl Sapper, a geographer related to the Sapper coffee entrepreneurs of the Verapaz, is also included. One of the IIN's first publications was Leonhard Schultze Jena's ethnography, translated from the German and published as *La vida y las creencias de los indígenas quichés de Guatemala* (1954). Another early IIN project was the creation of a linguistic map, directed by Goubaud and based on Otto Stoll's work.

His 1945 literature review bears the mark of his immersion in U.S. anthropology, however. While respectful of the German scholars' accomplishments, Goubaud describes their methods with the usual U.S. anthropologists' critique of their interest in reconstructing a pseudouniversal history, à la Gumplowicz, Lubbock, Tylor, Morgan, and Spencer (1945b).

His essay reflects the shift in U.S. anthropology underway as he began high school at St. Mary's College in California's Bay area. The teenager Goubaud would have been unaware of the first rumblings against the unified Boasian field, of course, but these were to have a big impact on his own formation as an anthropologist. A. L. Kroeber, Ishi's sponsor and one of Franz Boas's first anthropology doctorates, left the Bay area on sabbatical the year Goubaud arrived. That marked the end of fifteen years spent researching the small decimated groups of California Indians, largely through interviews with "survivors." In Kroeber's words, it was the end of years of writing "the little history of pitiful events" (Buckley 1996: 259).

When Kroeber returned from sabbatical, his anthropology turned sharply from Boas's historical particularism and toward grand theory. He began work with the highly organized, vibrant Pueblo peoples. Goubaud and later David Vela would visit these vital societies, albeit during wartime in which many Pueblo young men were overseas fighting for the Allies. These provided Goubaud and Vela with an important example of a people, a "nation," maintaining itself and its peoples as members of another nation.

Kroeber, like Goubaud, had been raised in a German expatriate culture, for

Kroeber the bourgeois and artistic Deutschamerikanish elite of nineteenth-century Manhattan. This tight-knit, demanding community promoted humanism, literature, and the arts in its own learned circles, and worshiped "science" and the "ice cold flame of passion of truth for truth's sake" (Buckley 1996, citing Boas and Stocking 1974: 22).[29] Kroeber, after 1915, would return to the themes of the rise and fall of civilizations, the Superorganic. These themes were the themes of Guatemala's debate, and Goubaud would be among the few Guatemalans aware of the debate in anthropology.

When Goubaud took a semester at Harvard in the mid-1930s, he immersed himself in a university with a long history of work, archaeological and ethnological, in Mesoamerica. He also entered an intellectual environment in which synchronic studies of social structure and social relations would rule for several decades, deposing historical context and comparative religion. Goubaud, reading *American Anthropologist* and *American Ethnologist* and other publications regularly, was most drawn to the debates about individual psychology, cultural patterns, and social change, interests he shared with many of the U.S. anthropologists now arriving in Guatemala.

The Influence of Redfield and Tax

Goubaud was among many Latin American anthropologists directly influenced by Redfield. As research associate of the Carnegie Institution of Washington from 1930 through 1946, Redfield directed much funding toward ethnological and sociological investigations of the Maya peoples of the Yucatán, Mexico, and Guatemala. His personal contact with aspiring anthropologists in Mexico, Guatemala, and the United States shaped an entire generation and beyond. Redfield's theory of culture change, the "great dichotomy" between folk and urban societies, exposed all those who knew or read him to an intellectual framework with roots in European theorists such as Émile Durkheim, Henry James Sumner Maine, and Ferdinand Tonnies.

Redfield extended his work in Guatemala by sending anthropologist Solomon Tax there in 1934. Having met Goubaud in Guatemala, Tax excitedly wrote to Redfield that Goubaud was a "jewel for our purposes." Tax mentioned Redfield's relationship with Alfonso Villa Rojas, the young school teacher in Chan Kom, whom Redfield met in 1930, employed, and later mentored to a prestigious career as a top Mexican anthropologist. Tax described Goubaud as having made trips to the western highlands to study K'iche' and Kaqchikel Mayan, as having acquired "quite a library of Guatemalan history and ethnology, and as interested as anyone can be" (quoted in Rubinstein 2002: 45).

Tax wrote: "Naturally he respects my training; and naturally I consider him a find, both for future purposes (I think that you agree that part of our business is to develop natural resources, so to speak) and for the present work." Tax reported that Goubaud did not require any pay for accompanying the Carnegie researchers, but that his expenses should be covered and would not amount to much. He adds: "I think, therefore, that it would be very wise to take him under my wing as you took Alfonso [Villa Rojas] under yours. If it works out all right, I would—in the matter of publication—consider him a co-worker (you know I'm not the jealous kind)" (quoted in Rubinstein 2002: 45).

Redfield responded to the "find" with enthusiasm in a letter dated November 6, 1934: "Your letter about Goubaud bucked me up to no end. It sounds like too good a break to get so early in the game. If he turns out as well as you think he will, I am sure that to pay his expenses will be a good investment. You are authorized to try him on this basis. . . . I would make no promises to Goubaud about helping him in the future, but rather talk of Alfonso's experience and continue to stimulate his scientific interest and ambition. If he turns out well, of course something can be done for him, but he should not be told that directly" (quoted in Rubinstein 2002: 47).

Within six days, however, complications emerged that marked the rest of Tax's correspondence regarding Goubaud. Tax wrote to Redfield that "the news of the day is that Goubaud, although as anxious as ever to get into ethnological work with me, is not as available as I was at first led to believe." Tax mentioned some "vague family business" that required Goubaud's continued employment at Clark Tours. He discerned that the family was weathering some depression-era economics, with a few family fincas being sold. Yet Tax also thought the Goubaud family enjoyed a good life, with a "genteel" family home. He knew Goubaud's mother and brother were in the United States, "where the brother was in school." He wrote: "Two interpretations of the present situation are possible: either he is actually poor, has no hope of getting richer, made up this yarn about family affairs, and in fact can never expect to leave his job to become a student-ethnologist; or he is telling the truth, and in a month or two may be free, as he puts it, to do what he wishes" (quoted in Rubinstein 2002: 49).

Tax did not know that the "vague family business" was serious family illness: Goubaud's mother and brother were institutionalized in the United States. For the next five years, Goubaud kept in touch with Tax, networked for him, and provided him with books. Tax wrote letters to Redfield requesting funds for Goubaud. Redfield always replied cagily, presenting possibilities but with the stern order that Tax say nothing to Goubaud. At one point, in early 1935, Tax was authorized to offer Goubaud the same wages as the indigenous man, Tomás Ventura, an employee at Chichicastenango's Mayan Inn who also worked for Tax. Goubaud turned down the offer, again mentioning family problems.

"On the other hand," Tax wrote, "he will gladly go to the States for further training any time the opportunity offers (the sooner the better)" (quoted in Rubinstein 2002: 90). Goubaud kept his eyes on the prize: study at Chicago. Redfield remained cagey with his support, despite the favorable impression the Guatemalan made on Redfield's colleagues who traveled to Guatemala, among them Oliver Ricketson, Alfred Kidder, and Manuel Andrade.

Finally, in early 1939, Goubaud cleared the financial, familial, and academic obstacles preventing him from going to Chicago. On January 23, 1939, Redfield wrote to Tax that "I had a call recently from Antonio Goubaud. He says that he has resolved to become an anthropologist, and that in March he is coming to the University of Chicago to begin his training. He has to do the College work first. Apparently he expects to pay his way" (quoted in Rubinstein 2002: 258). Tax introduced one more whirl in the trio's odd dynamics, writing February 12, 1939: "Goubaud told me he doesn't think he'll be able to go to Chicago; I took the liberty of mentioning (since the question seemed to be financial) that we might have a little work, but of course I couldn't speak for the Institution. He gave me a reference to a local botany book that identified many local plants." Tax then writes, somewhat panicked, on March 5:

> I don't know if I mentioned to you that I talked to Goubaud, who is definitely coming to Chicago this Spring. In case you see him, here or there, you should know that I was forced into indiscreetly telling him (with due warnings that I have no power to do anything myself) something of our plan to use his assistance in preparing a Guatemalan glossary. I saw him one day and, as I told you, mentioned that he might hope for remunerative work in Chicago; I must have given the impression then that I knew what kind of work it would be, for several days later he came to the house excitedly asking what the project was. Rather than surround it in mystery and give it more importance than it deserves, I told him. (quoted in Rubinstein 2002: 272)

Goubaud reached Chicago on April 15, 1939. Two years later, in 1941, so did Juan de Dios Rosales, the Maya consultant who, as a local schoolteacher and cooperative, paid consultant, was more comparable to Villa Rojas than Goubaud. In April 1936, Tax "found" Rosales, who worked for a field season for Tax at the towns of Lake Atitlán. Rosales, who was in a second marriage to a ladina at the time of his meeting Redfield and Tax, emerged as a case study in Redfield and Tax's attempts to understand Guatemalan race relations (Rubinstein 2002: 172).

Rosales received considerable financial support to reach Chicago. Tax, Kidder, and Redfield worked with the Rockefeller Foundation, the University of Chicago, and the Carnegie Institution of Washington to sponsor Rosales.[30] When Rockefeller funding fell through, both Kidder and Redfield stepped in with the necessary funds. Redfield made housing and language study arrangements. Tax was given permission to "safely prepare Rosales for the event. This I did. He is of course much excited by the prospect. I cautioned him to silence and on my part have not told anyone. . . . I think that Goubaud should hear of Rosales' impending visit from you; there may come a time when he will find the technical assistance of Rosales very valuable. Don't you think it might be good psychology to ask Goubaud to take Rosales (who comes as an innocent to the big city) under his wing?" (quoted in Rubinstein 2002: 322).

The last mention of Goubaud in the published correspondence between Redfield and Tax is when Redfield writes, "Goubaud left last night for Cambridge, where a group of anthropologists are meeting tomorrow and Saturday to read papers on 'applied anthropology' and perhaps to organize a society of applied anthropologists. Kidder has some interest in it and I suggested that Goubaud attend" (quoted in Rubinstein 2002: 324).

Redfield and Tax's correspondence reflects several complex relationships in a complicated postwar geometry of race, nationality, academic empire building—and in Goubaud's case, the management of an elite family's secret. Goubaud did not have a straightforward patron-client relationship with either Redfield or Tax, as perhaps his nationalist twist calling for an end to foreign monopoly of research indicated. Goubaud politely rejected Redfield and Tax's first employment offer, for example, knowing quite well what people were paid in the United States and what Indians were paid in Guatemala. He mentioned "family problems," turned down demeaning offers, yet also remained on good terms with the U.S. academics. Redfield and Tax later promoted Goubaud's Chicago-side mentorship of Rosales, perhaps to soften the personal blow to Goubaud of the other Guatemalan's good fortunes.

Goubaud found his career stymied by Tax's and Redfield's hierarchical relationship. The letters from 1934 to 1941 indicate the growth of a closely reciprocated friendship, but one in which Redfield remained the senior colleague and intellectual leader. Whatever Tax's hopes for Goubaud were, he had little power in the relationship with Redfield to assert them. Tax later promoted "action anthropology" in his work with students, colleagues, and the field at large. Some of his efforts in this line were dubbed "Sollies' follies" by his Chicago colleagues behind his back.[31] He returned to Guatemala to do applied fieldwork with Goubaud and Rosales. While Redfield sent Goubaud to the conference on applied anthropology with the other colleagues, he himself was interested in theory, and had little interest in applied anthropology.[32]

Goubaud in the Maya Field: Alta Verapaz

In July 1944, Goubaud arrived in San Juan Chamelco, Alta Verapaz, as part of a comparative study of different Guatemalan towns, documenting the diets and food customs of ladinos and Mayas. Goubaud was directed by Tax and supported by the Carnegie Institute; I first encountered him through his field notes of this experience.

Goubaud spent the earlier part of 1944 in Jocotán, in the heart of the Ch'orti' Maya region. The months he spent there in the stifling heat and social oppression were unrewarding, relations between ladinos and Ch'orti' Mayas so exploitive as to be a caricature of the national conundrum referred to as the "Indian problem."

He then moved to work in Alta Verapaz, which he found a welcome contrast. He was enchanted by the beauty of San Juan Chamelco, and impressed by the Verapaz residents. He and his wife dreamed of retiring there. In many aspects, Chamelco resembled much of Guatemala. It was a municipality set in a region developed for export coffee cultivation by Germans. The coffee economy depended on indigenous labor. In both region and township, indigenous people had lost secure land tenure. Reviewing the 1944 municipal census, Goubaud found that only 334 of Chamelco's 18,245 inhabitants owned land, while 66 percent were registered as manual laborers. Ladinos owned all four stores and six butcher shops (Goubaud 1949d).

But Chamelco residents presented several anomalies. First, Goubaud noted a "minimum of friction between the two cultures . . . the tension between ladinos and Indians does exist, but so do mechanisms to keep these down" (Goubaud 1949d: 23). Many of the ladinos spoke Q'eqchi', even though their families had lived in the region for only a few generations. He noted that ladinos and Germans participated in Q'eqchi' *costumbre* (customs, traditions). They made pilgrimages to, and left offerings at, earth shrines. They consulted Q'eqchi' healers and diviners. He was struck by the stability and stature of the intermarriages of ladinos (both men and women) with Q'eqchi' partners.

Some of their children were considered ladinos and others Indian, but the designation followed no strict order of racial miscegenation.

Second, he was impressed by the culture of the town's economic specialty, tailoring, which seemed more open to outside influences, such as foreign evangelical missionaries. The indigenous tailors were no less Q'eqchi' in language, dress, and work ethic. Yet they seemed to be getting ahead. The richest man in town was an evangelical Protestant Q'eqchi' tailor.

Finally, Goubaud observed that indigenous people, the Q'eqchi' Mayas, led an active, vibrant life of *costumbre,* but they were also interested in events outside of their region; his chief consultant and others asked him for further news on World War II. They read news bulletins that one expatriate planter distributed weekly. They followed news of the capital's strikes and contra-Ubico activity.

In San Juan Chamelco, Goubaud followed up on his earlier interests in Maya spirituality, despite Tax's impatience with ritual life. He recorded several dream analyses related to him by Indians, noting the similarity of their process to psychoanalysis. He consulted one renowned spirit medium. He observed her professional, confident manner. She asked, in Q'eqchi' Mayan, for news of Ubico and of the German war. She was open and articulate in her instructions to Goubaud and in her responses to his questions. When she entered a trance, he described the experience as a genuine spiritual state. She accurately diagnosed his wife's homesickness.[33]

In summary, the experience in Alta Verapaz confirmed for Goubaud that, first, Mayas would respond immediately and positively to new technology and economic opportunity; second, that Maya people could follow *costumbre* and world news; third, that indigenous mentality on spiritual matters was not particularly "cloudy," certainly in comparison with the "whites" in town, who he found quite superstitious; and finally, that indigenous communities could respond to outsiders in ways that either channeled the "best" cultural traits or that reinforced the most destructive and exploitive aspects.

Conclusion

After the field experience in San Juan Chamelco and then, as the director of IIN, Goubaud could imagine a path to "modernity" for Guatemala that did not require an assimilated Maya population. His vision, however, is complicated, ambivalent, perhaps prefiguring some of the contradictions of late-twentieth-century multiculturalism discourses. He expresses the conflict between his intellectual formation and the pressing needs of the Guatemalan revolutionary project, when he describes his dilemma in his 1945 inaugural speech; he states that as a social anthropologist, he acknowledges the value of the world's different cultures. As a nation builder, however, he had to create a culture based on the unification and simplification of values. He was compromised by the framing of the nation-building debate within the discourse about "homogeneous nationality." Witness how Juárez Muñoz, a decade earlier facing the same constraining discourse, had coined the term "positive nationality" in order to argue his opposition to the vision of a "white" Guatemala.

Goubaud was very concerned with anthropological applications to Guatemala's revolution and to the problems he had witnessed in the countryside. In line with the *longue durée* of U.S. anthropology, his writing consistently debunks the legitimacy of any essentialist racial differences. By 1945 he had stopped describing indigenous mentality as any cloudier or more ignorant than that of other Guatemalans; instead, he describes members of "both" cultures, indigenous and nonindigenous, as being alienated from national symbols or citizen identity. Indigenous peoples, furthermore, had been deprived of national services such as education.

I argue that Goubaud envisioned a Guatemala in which a unifying nationalism could coexist with diverse local cultures and identities. There is no doubt that Goubaud wrote about the best means to promote change in indigenous communities, while preserving certain aspects of Indian culture. Indeed, in a later essay, he waxes visionary about the possibilities for Guatemala. Rather in keeping with the more mystical schools of German-inspired thinking about Indians, such as the theosophists, he constructs a visionary "culture history" for Mayas: he proposes a sixth stage to Oliver La Farge's famous historical periodization of five stages.[34] Goubaud's sixth stage would begin in 1945 and realize his optimistic multicultural scenario (1956: 144). The sixth stage was to be marked by increasing political involvement of indigenous peoples at the local level, by the government's commitment to social welfare above economic infrastructure, and by a general recognition of the importance of indigenous culture to the country's modern life.

Goubaud expressed the optimism of the years immediately following the overthrow of Ubico in 1944. Goubaud the IIN director regarded anthropology and government as a source of support to indigenous people. He advocated national sensitivity to local variation; he was in the midst of a revolution promoting local development. Government programs could help people develop a repertoire of cultural skills, retain their separate local identities, and participate fully as actors in the national economy and society. The IIN carried out a number of studies in rural communities on political and social economic organization. The IIN brought legal aid and political information into communities through brochures and "misiones ambulantes." The IIN developed various bilingual education projects.

He also asserted his intellectual confidence in challenges to Redfield's folk-urban dichotomy, and Tax's writings. One of Goubaud's first acts, following the strategy laid out in his IIN speech, was to order municipal township surveys of the definitions of *Indian*. The surveys revealed that there was no general agreement despite Tax's famous description of how Indians could be identified. The few criteria that did exist varied from department to department and were vague: "customs and habits," followed by language.[35] Goubaud advised redefining the national census methodology to reflect local variation. Exercising more cultural relativity than his U.S. anthropologist mentor, Tax, at this moment, he stressed that what counted in social life and structure were the "relations between members," rather than the contents of some a priori category.

He hired Mayas and ladinos as IIN researchers, realizing his vision of Guatemalan research for and by Guatemalans. He also hired and consulted with U.S. anthropologists (including African American anthropologists), many active in the first four years of the 1944 Revolution. But they worked within his vision for the IIN. Goubaud left the IIN directorship with a rigorously developed work plan for the institution. After his death, Joaquín Noval—the second director of the IIN, who was mentored by Goubaud and, like him, spent many months doing fieldwork in rural Guatemalan communities—expanded Goubaud's vision of the IIN (R. N. Adams 2000).[36]

One more relationship must be addressed: that between Goubaud and President Arévalo, who was two years younger than Goubaud. Goubaud and Arévalo both returned to Guatemala to serve their country. The president's overall platform would have resonated with Goubaud's principles, including his strong desire for reform, his nationalism, the respect for the FDR-inspired "square deal," and the desire to open education and national civic space across the countryside. Certainly Arévalo's tendency toward collectivism, toward respecting individual freedom but within the context of various collective interests and social order," would have fit well with the functionalist legacy of Goubaud's Chicago formation.[37]

There is no indication in Goubaud's writings that he shared the Rodo-inspired spiritual socialism of Arévalo.[38] But Arévalo was drawing on strong intellectual trends of the early twentieth century. These intellectual currents caught up Goubaud as well, who founded the IIN one year after requesting the spirit possession session in Chamelco. Furthermore, it seems that Arévalo's "spiritualism" found expression primarily in the heart-swelling "spirit" of civic participation that circulated everywhere in the wartime United States.

International diplomacy, interpreting one people to another, was a logical next intellectual step for Goubaud. He had spent much of his years as a young scholar translating foreigners' writings for Guatemalans. As director of the IIN he worked toward increasing mutual understanding between Guatemala's "two cultures," and the civic presence of indigenous peoples in their own nation. He was deeply motivated to promote a parallel "mutual understanding" between the United States and Guatemala. He welcomed many foreign scholars beginning research in Guatemala, and sent one, Richard N. Adams, to Guatemala.

He welcomed me to my new field site through the words and insight captured in his field notes, words that reached me fifty years later. A few years later, Guatemalan anthropologist Christa Little-Siebold shared with me his obituary and I learned the nature of his death. I have reached back over fifty years to understand his life and work better. Guatemalans (and Americans) lost so much irretrievably in the coup and post-coup era, but I hope that this fuller story of Goubaud recovers something that need not be lost: pride in his work and a resource as we move forward.

Acknowledgments

Thanks to Monica and Cristina Goubaud, who gave the biographical work of their father urgency and meaning and generously shared their contribution of priceless memories and documents. Lilliane Goubaud and Ricardo Pokorny Goubaud (his great-niece and -nephew), and other Goubaud Carrera relatives who requested confidentiality, were generous and informative. I particularly thank Goubaud Carrera's great-niece and Guatemalan intellectual historian Marta Casaús Arzú, who provided the opportunity for me to expand my interest in Goubaud Carrera, critiqued my drafts, supplied leads, nurtured me intellectually, and cared about her family's story. Rick Adams also read drafts, shared leads and context, and shared my interest in his older colleague's story. The alumni office of St. Mary's College made my archival work possible and then invited me back to campus to present on their distinguished alumnus. Christa Little-Siebold, Felipe Girón, Benjamin Paul, and Robert Rubinstein helped me understand how complicated Goubaud Carrera's story and standing are. Finally, many thanks to the University of Illinois at Urbana-Champaign for sponsoring the conference and the publication of this volume.

Notes

1. By that point, Goubaud's legacy was regarded in highly dichotomous perspectives, depending on one's intellectual genealogy. Students from the Universidad de San Carlos from the 1970s onward were taught to suspect Goubaud's U.S. connections, while students at the Universidad del Valle were taught to regard Goubaud as one of Guatemala's first academically prepared anthropologists.

2. See for example Edward Fischer (2001); Virginia Garrard-Burnett (1998); Gonzalez Ponciano (1999, 1998); Jim Handy (1994, 1984: 48–52); Kay Warren (1998).

3. Handy, for example, translates *malestar* as *illness* (1994: 48–52).

4. This intellectual history project has begun with the work done by others on Guatemalan anthropology's disciplinary history (see also R. N. Adams 1999, 2000; Fischer 2001; Hale 1999; Handy 1994; Mendez Dominguez 1975; Gonzalez Ponciano 1988, 1997, 1999; Rubinstein 2002; Smith 1999; Warren 1998).

5. Casaús Arzú's working definition of organic intellectual: "[Un pensador] que amalga y confiere coherencia a la red y sobre todo le asegura su perdurabilidad y su hegemonía" (1992). She is related to Goubaud.

6. See Goubaud, "Notes on San Juan Chamelco, Alta Verapaz" (1949d) and "Notes on the Indians of Eastern Guatemala" (1949e).

7. The spirit cult has deep historical roots in the region, and generations of its members interacted with Verapaz spiritualists, theosophists, German coffee planters, spiritual seekers, and amateur ethnologists. As such, the cult members were enmeshed in the countermodern turn toward the spiritualism and theosophy that entranced certain members of the Generación de 1920 (Casaús Arzú 2003).

8. One of their fincas, La Azotea in Jocotenango, now is the site of the Museo del Café, the Casa K'ojom, and a regional museum; it features a short family history and is directed by Goubaud's great-nephew, Ricardo Pokorny Goubaud.

9. Wright also figures prominently in *Silence on the Mountain,* when he makes the loan that saves a German coffee grower and his family from ruin (Wilkinson 2002).

10. Contrary to one author (Gonzalez Ponciano 1999), Goubaud did not attend a military academy. Founded in 1863 by the Roman Catholic Archdiocese of San Francisco, St. Mary's is now one of the oldest colleges in the U.S. West. In 1868, St. Mary's College came under the direction of the teaching order La Salle Christian Brothers. Information based on interviews conducted March 30, 2003, at St. Mary's College's Moraga campus. See also McDevitt 1963 and Web sites for St. Mary's College of California (www.stmarys-ca.edu), and for the Christian Brothers of La Salle (www.lasalle.org).

11. For example, the brothers received exiled Capuchin and Dominican priests from Guatemala in the 1870s.

12. Goubaud first appears in the account books in 1917, following a normal high school curriculum, sponsored by John Wright & Co., A. Gallegos, of 22 Battery Street,

San Francisco, through 1920. In 1920 and 1921, his parent or guardian was Mrs. Elana de Martinez, of 1111 Pine Street, San Francisco.

13. Graduation program, Department of Commerce, St. Mary's College, 1919.

14. For background on Ishi, see Heizer and Kroeber (1979); Riffe and Roberts (1994).

15. Fernandez Hall (1924), cited in Hendrickson (1997). The society's inaugural class included thirty men and three women, all from the urban, ladino elite of Guatemala and all with a fervent drive to create "purely scientific investigation," but also to end Guatemala's perceived isolation from the rest of the modern world. Another source is the society's own anniversary volume (1948).

16. Alfred Clark was a U.S. expatriate who established a number of successful businesses in Guatemala, in addition to Clark Tours. Redfield had given Tax a letter of introduction to Clark, whom he had met the previous year during a brief visit to Guatemala to arrange for further survey and ethnology (Rubinstein 2002: 42–43).

17. He wrote a report from the study (Goubaud Carrera 1942). He was sponsored by the Bureau of Indian Affairs (BIA), the Carnegie Institution of Washington, and Chicago's anthropology department.

18. Goubaud also worked on a project with Michel Pijoan, a BIA nutritional specialist, to promote Guatemalan fish farming and consumption (Gillin 1952; Vela 1956).

19. Gonzalez Ponciano (1997) and Handy (1994) erroneously report that Paul alone wrote the guide, implying U.S. control of Guatemalan research design.

20. R. N. Adams, speech upon accepting the LASA Kalman H. Silvert Award in September 1998 (R. N. Adams 1998).

21. Guatemala was the only country to request a placement, rather than be offered a placement (R. N. Adams 1998, personal communication).

22. Interviews (in addition to others who asked not to be cited): Benjamin Paul, August 1996; Lilliane Goubaud, 2003; Lilly Uribe 2003. See also Vela (1956).

23. See Vela's curriculum vita, presented in *También sueños* (1982) and other sources. Vela was born February 25, 1901, studied at the Instituto Nacional Central para Varones, graduated as a lawyer from the Universidad de San Carlos de Guatemala in 1926, was one of the thirteen founders of the Asociación Estudiantil Universitario (AEU) and of the Universidad Popular (Guatemala City) in 1922, and a member of the Club Unionista (see also Mendizábal 1993).

24. Note that while Vela appears all through Goubaud's life and even in Goubaud's chronology of Guatemalan ethnologists, the reverse is not true. Goubaud barely appears in *También sueños,* the festschrift collection of Vela's short stories and reflections published in 1982 in honor of Vela's eightieth birthday, or in other biographies of Vela. Vela, the energetic and enduring editor of *El Imparcial,* was involved in many friendships, networks, and institutions. Goubaud was one element in one area of the *sueños* that he realized (including, tragically, ending the revolution; Vela 1955).

25. Glorifying the Maya past in prose is a position shared by Generación de 1920 members of different racialist dispensations. Although Vela considered the con-

temporary descendants degraded peoples, he wrote a descriptive piece concerning K'iche' Maya marriage and kinship practices that makes no mention of degradation or inbreeding practices. "Un Viejo Maya" is the title that Vela gives to an appreciation of German coffee entrepreneur and fellow Sociedad de Geografía e Historia member E. P. Dieseldorff (1940).

26. At the end of the series, Aceña Duran returned to Guatemala City, and *El Imparcial*'s editors published teasing commentary and a photograph of him dressed in the men's clothing of Todos Santos.

27. See Stocking (1996) and Lloyd (1991). Lloyd addresses the "speed and drama" with which the newly constituted German nation confronted modernization at the end of the nineteenth century, and how this pace heightened the dilemmas and contradictions of the look backward and the look forward. German fascination with indigenous peoples and with primitivism projected the counter-modernization project into German ethnology (Lloyd 1991, vi–x), creating a boom in ethnological museums, complete with imported living subjects.

28. This essay was widely cited by other bibliographers of Guatemalan anthropology (Casey 1979; Eggan 1968; Ewald 1956).

29. Boas, of course, was raised in Germany. He and his U.S. intellectual descendants all read German works routinely in their studies and courses, and they imported and transformed methods and questions derived directly from European antiquarianism, the assumptions of ethnology (or the pursuit of a history of a people), and the techniques of diffusionism (or cultural diversity across space, particularly as initiated by the work of Ratzel) (Bunzel 1960: 400–402).

30. See Stocking (1991) for a discussion of the Rockefeller influence on U.S. anthropology.

31. Robert Rubinstein, personal communication, February 2003.

32. See, for example, Redfield (1958).

33. Many thanks to Monica and Cristina Goubaud for access to their mother's diaries of this fieldwork.

34. La Farge, a novelist and U.S. ethnographer of Jacaltenango in the 1920s, had been invited to Guatemala by the Carnegie Institution (see LaFarge 1940, 1930).

35. See Tax (1937) and Goubaud (1946e).

36. Noval added a study of rural credit access, a joint project with the Panamerican Union to develop an archive for research and data concerning indigenous society, and the creation of an active bilingual literacy program for monolingual indigenous peoples (R. N. Adams 2000).

37. See Handy (1994: 86).

38. José Enrique Rodo (1988) argued that unlike the materially driven societies of the North Atlantic, Latin people were grounded in spiritual motives; this, he suggested, ultimately promised a type of higher development that fused practical Yankee know-how with sublime principles.

Works Cited

Aceña Duran, Ramón

1939   El indio incognito. El Imparcial January 3:3.

Adams, Abigail E.

1996   Exception, Rule, Proof?: Antonio Goubaud Carrera, San Juan Chamelco and the National Indigenous Institute. Paper presented at With an Eye on the Ancestors, invited session, American Anthropological Association, San Francisco, November 20–24.

1999   Los cultos de posesión, la Rigoberta Menchú y el Rabin Ajau: El género y la tradición de entrar en trance en las culturas mayas. *In* Memorias del Segundo Congreso Internacional sobre *El Pop Wuj*. Quetzaltenango, Guatemala: Centro de Estudios Mayas, Timach.

2001   Making One Our Word: Evangelical Q'eqchi' Mayans in Highland Guatemala. *In* Holy Saints and Fiery Preachers: The Anthropology of Protestantism in Mexico and Central America. J. W. Dow and A. R. Sandstrom, eds. Pp. 205–234. Westport, Conn.: Praeger Press.

2008   Cultural Diversity in National Homogeneity?: Antonio Goubaud Carrera and the "Founding of Guatemala's Instituto Indigenista Nacional." Mesoamerica 50:66–95.

2009   Reviving Our Spirits: Revelation, *Re-encuentro* and *Retroceso* in Post Accords Verapaz. *In* Mayas in Postwar Guatemala: *Harvest of Violence* Revisited. Walter E. Little and Timothy J. Smith, eds. Pp. 30–41. Tuscaloosa: University of Alabama Press.

Adams, Richard N.

1998   Richocheting through a Half-Century of Revolution. LASA Forum 24(3) Fall: 14–20.

1999   De la hegemonía a la antihegemonía: Racismo y antropología estadounidense en Guatemala. *In* Racismo en Guatemala? Abriendo el debate sobre un tema tabú. Clara Arenas Bianchi, Charles R. Hale, and Gustavo Palma Murga, eds. Pp. 127–191. Guatemala: AVANCSO.

2000   Joaquín Noval como indigenista, antropólogo y revolucionario. Guatemala: Cuadernos de Pensamiento Universitario, Editorial Universitaria.

Arévalo Bermejo, Juan José

1945   Escritos Politicos. Guatemala: Tipografía Nacional.

Arriola, Aura Marina

1995   La cuestión étnica en la revolución de octubre. Jaguar-Venado, Revista guatemalteca de cultura y política (Mexico) 1(3):29–31.

Asturias, Miguel Angel

1923   Sociología guatemalteca: el problema social del indio. Guatemala: USAC.

Boas, Franz, and George Stocking, ed.

1974   A Franz Boas Reader: The Shaping of American Anthropology, 1883–1911. Chicago: University of Chicago Press.

Buckley, Thomas
  1996 The Little History of Pitiful Events: The Epistemological and Moral Contexts of Kroeber's California Ethnology. *In* Volksgeist as Method and Ethic: Essays on Boasian Ethnography and the German Anthropological Tradition. George Stocking Jr., ed. Pp. 257–297. Madison: University of Wisconsin Press.

Bunzel, Ruth
  1960 Introduction. *In* The Golden Age of American Anthropology. Margaret Mead and Ruth Bunzel, eds. Pp. 400–402. New York: George Braziller.

Campbell, Bruce F.
  1980 Ancient Wisdom: A History of the Theosophical Movement. Berkeley: University of California Press.

Casaús Arzú, Marta Elena
  1992 Guatemala: linaje y racismo. San José, Costa Rica: FLACSO.
  2001 Los elites intelectuales y la generación del 20 en Guatemala: Su vision del indio y su imaginario de nación. *In* Historia Intelectual de Guatemala. Marta Elena Casaús Arzú and Oscar Guillermo Peláez Almengor, eds. Pp. 1–50. Guatemala: Universidad de San Carlos.
  2003 La influencia de la teosofía en las redes intelectuales de la década del 20: La regeneración de la nación y la redención del indio. Paper presented for panel Las redes intelectuales en la década del 20 y la formación de la nación en Guatemala. Latin American Studies Association, Dallas.
  2005 Las redes intelectuales centroamericanas: un siglo de imaginarios nacionales (1820–1920). Guatemala: F&G Editoriales.

Casey, Dennis
  1979 "Indigenismo: The Guatemalan Experience." Ph.D. dissertation, University of Kansas.

Deves Valdes, Eduardo, and Ricardo Melgar Bao
  1999 Redes teosóficas y pensadores políticos latinoamericanos 1910–1930. Cuadernos americanos 78:137–152.

Eggan, Fred
  1968 One Hundred Years of Ethnology and Social Anthropology. *In* One Hundred Years of Anthropology. J. O. Brew, ed. Pp. 119–149. Cambridge, Mass.: Harvard University Press.

Ewald, Robert H.
  1956 Bibliografía comentada sobre antropología social guatemalteca, 1900–1955. Guatemala: Seminario de Integración Social Guatemalteco.

Fernandez Hall, Francisco
  1924 Organización y labores de la Sociedad de Geografía e Historia. Anales de la Sociedad de Geografía e Historia de Guatemala 1(1):19–22.

Fischer, Edward F.
  2001 Cultural Logics and Global Economies: Maya Identity in Thought and Practice. Austin: University of Texas Press.

Forster, Cindy
2001   The Time of Freedom: Campesino Workers in Guatemala's October Revolution. Pittsburgh: University of Pittsburgh Press.
Gamio, Manuel
1960   Forjando patria. México: Editorial Porrua.
Garcia Giraldez, Teresa
2003   El debate sobre la patria grande: unionismo y panamericanismo en la década del 20. Paper presented for panel Las redes intelectuales en la década del 20 y la formación de la nación en Guatemala. Latin American Studies Association, Dallas.
Garrard-Burnett, Virginia
1998   Protestantism in Guatemala: Living in the New Jerusalem. Austin: University of Texas Press.
Gillin, John Philip
1952a   Ethos and Cultural Aspects of Personality. In Heritage of Conquest. Sol Tax, ed. Pp. 193–224. Glencoe, Ill: Free Press.
1952b   Obituary, Antonio Goubaud Carrera, 1902–1951. American Anthropologist 54:71–73.
Gonzalez Ponciano, Jorge Ramón
1988   Diez años de indigenismo en Guatemala: la primera época del Instituto Indigenista Nacional (1944–1954). México: Escuela Nacional de Antropología e Historia.
1999   "Esas sangres no estan limpias," Modernidad y pensamiento civilizatorio en Guatemala (1954–1997). In Racismo en Guatemala? Abriendo el debate sobre un tema tabú. Pp. 15–46. Guatemala: AVANCSO.
Goubaud Carrera, Antonio
1935   El "Guajxaquip Bats": una ceremonia calendrica de los Maya-Quiche. Anales de la Sociedad de Geografía e Historia de Guatemala 12(1):39–52.
1937   The Guajxaquip Bats: An Indian Ceremony of Guatemala. Guatemala: Centro Editorial.
1938a   Opinion of the Geographical and Historical Society of Guatemala on Guatemala's Right to British Honduras. Translated from Spanish with Robert E. Smith. Guatemala: Sociedad de Geografía e Historia de Guatemala.
1938b   Prólogo. In Etnografía de la República de Guatemala. Translation of Zur Ethnographie der Republik Guatemala (Otto Stoll, 1884). Guatemala: Sanchez y de Guise.
1942   The Food Culture of Canyon de Taos, New Mexico. Report, Bureau of Indian Affairs: Washington, D.C.
1943   "Food Patterns and Nutrition in Two Spanish-American Communities." Master's thesis, Chicago: University of Chicago.
1945a   Adaptación del indígena a la cultura nacional moderna. Reprinted in Indigenismo en Guatemala. Guatemala: Centro Editorial José de Piñeda Ibarra.

1945b Del conocimiento del indio Guatemalteco. Revista de Guatemala 1(1). *Reprinted in* Indigenismo en Guatemala. Guatemala: Centro Editorial José de Piñeda Ibarra.

1945c Indigenismo guatemalteco. Inaugural address of IIN. *In* Indigenismo en Guatemala. Guatemala: Centro Editorial José de Piñeda Ibarra.

1946a Distribución de las lenguas indígenas actuales de Guatemala. Boletín del Instituto Indigenista Nacional 1(203). *Reprinted in* Indigenismo en Guatemala. Guatemala: Centro Editorial José de Piñeda Ibarra.

1946b El grupo étnico-indígena: criterios para su definición. Boletín del Instituto Indigenista Nacional 1–2:9–26. *Reprinted in* Indigenismo en Guatemala. Guatemala: Centro Editorial José de Piñeda Ibarra.

1946c Estudio de la alimentación en Guatemala. Boletín del Instituto Indigenista Nacional 1–2. *Reprinted in* Indigenismo en Guatemala. Guatemala: Centro Editorial José de Piñeda Ibarra.

1946d La nueva escuela rural. Boletín del Instituto Indigenista Nacional 2 (March–June):53–56.

1946e (with Herbert D. Sapper). Leonhard Schultze Jena, La vida y las creencias de los indígenas Quichés de Guatemala. Publicaciones Especiales del IIN. Guatemala. *Previously published in* Anales de la Sociedad de Geografía e Historia 20(1–4):1945.

1946f Reconnaisance of Northern Guatemala, from 1944. Manuscripts in Microfilm Collection of Manuscripts on Middle American Anthropology, Cultural Anthropology, 4th series, no. 23. Chicago: University of Chicago.

1948 Notes on the Indians of the finca Nueva Granada. Manuscripts in Microfilm Collection of Manuscripts on Middle American Anthropology, Cultural Anthropology, 4th series, no. 23. Chicago: University of Chicago.

1949a Algunos aspectos de la estructura del carácter de los indios de Guatemala. *In* Indigenismo en Guatemala. Guatemala: Centro Editorial José de Piñeda Ibarra.

1949b Idiomas indígenas de Guatemala. Guatemala: Instituto de Antropología e Historia.

1949c "Notes on San Juan Chamelco, Alta Verapaz." Manuscripts in Microfilm Collection of Manuscripts on Middle American Anthropology, Cultural Anthropology, 4th series, no. 23. Chicago: University of Chicago.

1949d "Notes on the Indians of Eastern Guatemala." Manuscripts in Microfilm Collection of Manuscripts on Middle American Anthropology, Cultural Anthropology, 4th series, no. 23. Chicago: University of Chicago.

1949e Problemas etnológicos del Popol Vuh. Revista Antropología e Historia de Guatemala 1(1):35–42. *Reprinted in* Indigenismo en Guatemala. Guatemala: Centro Editorial José de Piñeda Ibarra.

1956 Indigenismo en Guatemala. Guatemala: Centro Editorial José de Piñeda Ibarra.

Grandin, Greg
  2004   The Last Colonial Massacre: Latin America in the Cold War. Chicago: University of Chicago Press.
Hale, Charles R.
  1999   El discurso ladino del racismo al revés en Guatemala. *In* Racismo en Guatemala? Abriendo el debate sobre un tema tabú. Clara Arenas Bianchi, Charles R. Hale, and Gustavo Palma Murga, eds. Pp. 273–304. Guatemala: AVANCSO.
Handy, Jim
  1984   Gift of the Devil: A History of Guatemala. Boston: South End Press.
  1994   Revolution in the Countryside: Rural Conflict and Agrarian Reform in Guatemala, 1944–1954. Chapel Hill: University of North Carolina Press.
Heizer, Robert F., and Theodora Kroeber, eds.
  1979   Ishi the Last Yahi: A Documentary History. Berkeley: University of California Press.
Hendrickson, Carol
  1997   25 July 1924: Scholarship, Civilization, National Agendas, and the Place of Indians in Guatemala's IV Centenario Celebrations. Lecture, January 16, 1997, Dartmouth College.
La Farge, Oliver
  1930   The Ceremonial Year at Jacaltenango. Proceedings of the 23rd International Congress of Americanists. Pp. 659–660. New York.
  1940   Maya Ethnology: The Sequence of Cultures. *In* The Maya and Their Neighbors. C. L. Hay, eds. Pp. 281–291. New York: Appleton-Century.
Lloyd, Jill
  1991   German Expressionism: Primitivism and Modernity. New Haven, Conn.: Yale University Press.
Marroquin, Alejandro
  1972   Panoramo del indigenismo en Guatemala. America Indígena 32(2):291–317.
McDevitt, Matthew, Brother
  1963   The First Century of St. Mary's College (1863–1963). Moraga, Calif.: St. Mary's College.
Mendez Dominguez, Alfredo
  1975   Big and Little Traditions in Guatemalan Anthropology. Current Anthropology 16(4):541–552.
Mendizábal, Julio R.
  1993   David Vela: un perfil biográfico. Guatemala: Codelace.
Mendoza, Edgar S. G.
  1994   La arqueología en Guatemala: Antonio Goubaud Carrera; cuatro páginas de su Diario de Campo–13 de noviembre de 1943. Estudios: 26–36.

Nelson, Diane
  1999   A Finger in the Wound. Berkeley: University of California Press.
Redfield, Robert
  1958   Values in Action: A Comment. Human Organization 18(1). *Reprinted in*
          Human Nature and the Study of Society: The Papers of Robert Redfield,
          1962. Margaret Park Redfield, ed. Chicago: University of Chicago Press.
Riffe, Jed, and Pamela Roberts, producers and directors
  1994   Ishi, the Last Yahi. Film. Boston: WGBH, The American Experience.
Rodríguez Beteta, Virgilio
  1924   Discurso. Anales de la Sociedad de Geografía e Historia de Guatemala
          1(2):124–130.
Rodó, José E.
  1988[1900]   Ariel. Austin: University of Texas Press.
Rubinstein, Robert, ed.
  2002   Doing Fieldwork: The Correspondence of Robert Redfield and Sol Tax.
          Brunswick, N.J.: Transaction.
Smith, Carol A., ed.
  1990   Guatemalan Indians and the State: 1540–1988. Austin: University of Texas
          Press.
Smith, Carol A.
  1999   Interpretaciones norteamericanas sobre la raza y el racismo en Guatemala:
          una genealogía crítica. *In* Racismo en Guatemala? Abriendo el debate sobre
          un tema tabú. Pp. 93–126. Guatemala: AVANCSO.
Stocking, George
  1996   Volksgeist as Method and Ethic. Madison: University of Wisconsin Press.
  1991   The Ethnographer's Magic and Other Essays in the History of Anthropol-
          ogy. Madison: University of Wisconsin Press.
Tax, Sol
  1937   The Municipio of the Western Highlands. American Anthropologist.
  1941   World View and Social Relations in Guatemala. American Anthropologist
          43:27–42.
  1942   Ethnic Relations in Guatemala. America Indígena 2(4):43–48.
Vela, David
  1955   Prólogo. *In* Tácticas rojas en las Americas *by Daniel James.* México: Edito-
          rial Intercontinental.
  1956   Prólogo. *In* Indigenismo en Guatemala. Guatemala: Centro Editorial José
          de Piñeda Ibarra.
  1982   También sueños. Guatemala: Editorial Universitaria.
Warren, Kay B.
  1998   Indigenous Movements and Their Critics: Pan-Maya Activism in Guate-
          mala. Princeton, N.J.: Princeton University Press.
Wilkinson, Daniel
  2002   Silence on the Mountain: Stories of Terror, Betrayal, and Forgetting in
          Guatemala. Boston: Houghton Mifflin.

2

Recovering the Truth
of the 1954 Coup
Restoring Peace with Justice

JUNE C. NASH

During my student days in the 1950s, issues such as rebellions, coups, domestic violence, alcoholism, drugs, and corruption in public office were considered peripheral to the field project of anthropology; today they have become central to ethnography. And yet there were precedents to the focus on social conflict: Max Gluckman (1940) recognized the importance of conflicts and dysfunction as essential aspects of field analysis.[1] The subtitle to his later anthology *Open Minds and Closed Systems: The Limits of Naïveté in Social Anthropology* (Gluckman 1964) highlights a key issue in the development of social anthropology—that is, the need to cultivate a broader horizon in engaged fieldwork—which I consider here.

My first venture into fieldwork was in 1953, when the discipline of anthropology was still a field of discovery. At the time, anthropologists went into field situations largely innocent of the plots spawned in the emergent U.S. empire and of the role that we might unconsciously play as agents of an imperial power. The ethnographic frame was the functioning of traditional societies and the structures that maintained coherence in the face of changes related to modernity. Theoretical premises of the discipline in cultural relativism and holism proscribed the comparative assessment of social processes taking into account the global processes set into motion by an imperial framework of analysis.

The Chosen Place, the Timeless People

My husband Manning and I arrived in Guatemala in 1953 when the country was still experiencing the spring of democracy brought about by the revolution of 1944. The place chosen for my fieldwork was Cantel, and the timeless people were workers in the Cantel Fábrica de Textiles, one of the few factories operating in Guatemala.[2] In his survey of the western highlands of Guatemala in the 1930s, our professor, Sol Tax, had passed through Cantel. He was impressed by his view of a workforce made up of indigenous men and women working in a modern factory that employed some eight hundred hands. Fifteen years later, when we arrived we were also awed by our view of men and women wearing regional attire pouring out of the factory gates to cross a hammock bridge and climb the five hundred feet to Cantel village, high above the river. There at least half the workers lived in adobe brick houses with tile or thatched roofs, typical of those found throughout western highlands, and as many more lived in housing provided by the Basque owners, the Ibargüen family, near the factory.

Cantel was considered to be the center of the world by the people living in the municipal *cabecera* (town center). When we asked what proof they had, one of the volunteer policemen remarked that the sun was directly overhead at noon. Although the town was connected by a dirt road and a half-dozen taxis provided service to the departmental capital of Quetzaltenango, it was a culturally distinct entity, with women's *huipiles* embroidered with regional designs and the regional skirt material from Totonicapán draped in their own style. Only a couple of ladino families, including the school teacher and the pharmacist, lived in the village. K'iche' was spoken by all, and some were monolingual.

We soon learned of the social conflicts in the town and the factory compound below as we became engaged in the intricate balance among Indians and ladinos, or acculturated Indians, and mestizos, or mixed blood, and among social classes, which spanned the ethnic strata. While looking for a house to rent, we lived in the schoolhouse, since it was still during summer vacation. Our landlady, an Indian woman who was the first in her family to make the transition to ladino (non-Indian) status, was a curer. Since she was the lover of the ladino drugstore owner, we had the full gamut of medical lore open to us. The plant manager was the illegitimate son of one of the Ibargüen brothers. As a mestizo who had lived his early years with his mother in the village—until his father's wife spotted the resemblance to the Ibargüens and brought him to live in the big house—he was considered by many to merely feign sympathy for the union members who had organized the plant.[3] The heads of each of the three factory departments were foreigners: a Yorkshire weaving master and a Lancashire spinning master who were at odds with each other, and a German dyeing master. We at first assumed that the animosity between the only English speakers, whose families did not speak to each other, derived from ethnic grievances still alive after World War II, but later we learned that it was because the Yorkshire weaving master had refused to share with the Lancashire family the quota of lard available for Europeans when supplies were tight in the commissary.

Looking back on our imposed categories of what was traditional and what was modern, it is now clear to me that the mediators were those marginalized by miscegenation and extralegal reproduction. The ambiguities these aberrations created were not part of our ethnographic frame. Other divisions occurring in the workforce and in the village governance were more predictable in terms of structural factors in a traditional-to-modern paradigm defined by ethnicity, religion, class, and education. The revolutionary government of Juan José Arévalo had succeeded in its objectives of educating many indigenous youths, with the result that literate young men were working as mechanics and on maintenance crews. They were the leaders of the first union ever allowed in the factory. They were also challenging government officials in the pueblo. As a result of his military conscription, the mayor of the town, Santiago Xitimul, was one of the few literate members of his generation. A practicing Protestant before his election, he found himself obliged to drink during his tenure because of the many ceremonial occasions in which he was officially engaged as mayor, and vowed to return to abstinence after his term.

We learned of the opposition between Protestants and Catholics on the very first day of our arrival. Placards in the plaza announced "Aquí no hay protestantes! Los que vienen a proseletizar tienen que salir" (There are no Protestants here! Those who come to proselytize must leave). Apparently this threat was not scrupulously acted upon, as I learned later in my census of residents: there were more than five hundred converts to one or another of the three faiths actively converting Indians to Seventh-day Adventist, Presbyterian, and Jehovah's Witness (M. Nash 1958). They operated openly in the town center, relying on indigenous pastors to disseminate the Word of God with translations of the Bible into K'iche'. Their most fervent followers were women, who hoped that their husbands would, through conversion, become abstemious.

The greatest conflict however, was between traditional and catechist—orthodox, schooled—Catholics. During the previous decade of turbulent change the church had attempted to introduce a new orthodoxy and was actively proselytizing in an area where few priests had served in the past two hundred years. The Spanish priest, who had arrived from a parish in China to serve in Cantel just a few years before we arrived, remarked that he had never seen the level of poverty he encountered in the Guatemala highlands. Our rental house was only two blocks from the *cofradía* (brotherhood) residence of San Simón, identified with Judas, the anti-Christ and most powerful spiritual guide of the traditionalists.

There were also class divisions among indigenous agriculturalists. Two large landowners who occupied two-story houses in the plaza hired from thirty to forty campesinos to help cultivate the corn that was harvested in August, the month we arrived. They were afraid that the new land reform law might affect their holdings, and they, along with the factory owners, were actively protesting the new democracy. A distinctive sign of their wealth was their greater consumption of food, especially meat, evident in their greater girth and that of their wives. A second indicator was the large cohort of hired hands they employed during the harvest. These class differences among indigenous people had not yet been consolidated beyond community boundaries, although European and mestizo elites were nationally integrated.

The Coup and Its Aftermath

Our year of research was coming to an end in the summer of 1954 when rumors began to circulate about a rebellion led by Colonel Castillo Armas with five hundred armed soldiers, including former soldiers of the Wehrmacht, who had returned to claim the lands taken from families of German plantation owners during World War II. Castillo Armas had, as he later acknowledged, benefited from a Fort Leavenworth, Kansas, postgraduate training tour in preparation for his role as liberator. The U.S. *Radio Liberación* program broadcast ominous reports of the battles fought by these rebels, of the body count, and of poisoned lake water, but Manning and I tended to ignore them since such reports often proved false. We were somewhat more disturbed when government security agents arrived one day to a hamlet we were visiting, inquiring about our activities in the town. The mayor and Indian policemen told them that there were no gringos in town and offered no information regarding where we might be. This made us feel accepted by the villagers but still uneasy about national developments.

People became alarmed in June 1954 when airplanes began to circle overhead, apparently observing activities in the factory compound and the village. Cantel was suspect because of its workers union, and the suspicion that this represented a communist conspiracy. Daily *Radio Liberación* broadcasts warned of the massive rebellion forming in Honduras that was moving toward Guatemala. The workers camouflaged with evergreens the new steel and concrete bridge, which had replaced the precarious hammock bridge, in fear that this link from the factory to the town center would be bombed. Later, in June 1954, when Manning and I had just returned from Quetzaltenango, about ten kilometers distance from Cantel, *Radio Liberación* announced that there had been a skirmish between the rebels and government troops. Yet we had seen no signs of disturbance or any military troops.

On June 25 we decided to break the monotony of village life by going to a movie in Quetzaltenango. Youths with whom Manning played soccer joined us in the yellow jeep that we had bought secondhand. When we found the theater empty, we suspected that the uprising was something more than a rumor. We sat through the film despite the cold, without the body heat of the usual scores of Indians and ladinos. On our return we found trucks parked bumper to bumper as they loaded up campesinos recruited to defend the revolution. A lieutenant hailed a ride with us in our overloaded jeep, since he wanted to go to the head truck to account for the recruitment levels to his superior officer. We were afraid the army might commandeer the jeep because of the scarcity of vehicles, but he simply thanked us and took off, allowing us to return to Cantel center.

The next morning, June 26, 1954, we learned that the "war" was over while listening to *Radio Liberación*. Jack Peurifoy, the U.S. ambassador to Guatemala who had returned the night before from a "successful eradication of communism in Greece," had met with Arbenz, who pledged to avoid a bloodbath by leaving the country. The arms Arbenz had ordered from Czechoslovakia remained on a ship moored in the Gulf of Mexico, unable to dock because U.S. fighter planes hovered over the port. We could verify that the arms were never delivered to the countryside, where peasants mounted in trucks on the road to Cantel had only their machetes to defend *la patria*.[4] The presence of a Soviet allied ship loaded with arms provided the motivation for the Dulles brothers, who occupied the positions of secretary of state and head of the Central Intelligence Agency (CIA), to trigger the coup plot. Castillo Armas was seated as president on July 8, 1954.

Our friend, the union organizer, left Cantel the following day. We heard from reporters in Guatemala City that Arbenz had left the country, declaring that he took nothing with him. The next day *El Imparcial* had a front-page picture showing him passing through customs, his chest bared and his hands raised over his head as he was being searched. Not long afterward, our friends in the press corps indicated that a leading figure in Arbenz's diplomatic corps had used diplomatic immunity to withdraw a million U.S. dollars in small bills from the Guatemalan state bank. It was one of many stories that were never published. Another story appeared in *Time* magazine by one of their stringers, Harvey Rosenhouse, relating that the new president, Castillo Armas, had seized the corn sold by Mexicans at a low price to provide relief for peasants whose crops been trampled when the former owners took back their land, and was reselling them at high markups. In retribution, the government issued an order for troops to find and beat a journalist, "Herbert" Rosenhouse (a typical Guatemalan police error). Since Harvey had a twin brother Robert, Guatemalan intelligence had confused the target, calling him Herbert and capturing Robert instead. The latter was happy to report that he survived the beating since the clubs made in Guatemala broke before his head did. He escaped wounded but alive.

It was the beginning of low-intensity warfare backed by a U.S. naval blockade and CIA bombing runs out of Managua (Hersh 1992: 353) and the end of the imaginary timeless people. The coup was a testing operation for future interventions that continued throughout Central America except for a brief interlude during Jimmy Carter's presidency, when diplomatic steps were taken to end the blockade in Cuba and to forestall military intervention in Panama. In the days following the coup, rumors circulated about who was being jailed and who had fled.

The jails were filled with five thousand suspects when Richard Adams received a grant to study the penetration of Communist ideology in the countryside. He asked us to assist him, assigning Manning Nash and a number of Guatemalan students to the jail interviews and me to the compilation of results. Among the prisoners was a student who advised the team about the prisoners' interpretation of the questionnaire. Convinced that the interviews were part of a scheme to distinguish militant communists from those who were apolitical, the prisoners had worked out responses that minimized their involvement in the revolutionary government; our summation of the interviews confirmed this strategy. But the moderate views they expressed reflected a well-grounded support for the Arévalo-Arbenz government that was not based on fomenting a violent revolution. This, however, was the allegation of the U.S. National Security Council when it approved the plans for a coup against a government that had for the first time in Guatemalan history made strides in advancing rural education and health, and that had permitted democratic participation in unions and cooperatives.

In the following months, factory managers returned to their old practices. The weaving and spinning masters resumed their abusive labor practices, even hitting workers as they had done before there was a union. The weaving master denounced Manning and me as Communists to the U.S. embassy, but with the intervention of friends who spoke up we were not forced to leave. The entire embassy staff changed in the early months after the coup: the Spanish speakers knowledgeable of the country and of indigenous culture that we had known were gone, replaced by bridge-playing monolinguals who did not venture far from Guatemala City.

In August my husband and I took a break from fieldwork to go to Tiquisate, a major site of the United Fruit Company, in the low coastal plain. We stayed in one of the guest cottages maintained by the company. When we arrived, U.S. employees were still in a state of shock from the coup. They told us that U.S. airplanes had dropped caches of weapons for them to defend the company holdings, but they had fallen outside the gates, where the workers had seized them. Although they were not, as they had expected, held hostage or killed by insurgents, they attributed their salvation to God's intervention. Most social activities were suspended as though they were still in a state of siege, and we spent our days reading and relaxing in the warm comfort of the lower altitudes. We took our hosts' advice, taking walks only within the compound, on the endless roads lined by banana groves. It was an incongruous time heightened by my reading R. C. Hutchinson's novel of social workers in London slum life, *Elephant and Castle,* which had been left behind by a former guest.

Although we suspected that the company was involved in the coup, it was decades later that I learned of how Secretary of State John Foster Dulles, a major shareholder in the United Fruit Company, had promoted the coup because of the fear of land takeovers (Hersh 1992). He wired Castillo Armas when he took office at the end of July 1954 that "Communists should be considered [a] class additional to common criminals not entitled [to] asylum," and demanded that they be "convicted of having been covert Moscow agents" (Hersh 1992: 353).

When we returned to Chicago in 1954 we received an unexpected visit from a CIA agent on an extremely hot Indian summer day. He arrived one morning at the door of our basement apartment asking to see Manning Nash. At my invitation, he sat down, uncomfortably hot, dressed as he was in a tie and jacket, in the stuffy room next to the roaring furnace, fingering his briefcase as he waited for Manning to get up. It was a long, hot wait, with the furnace burning the accumulated trash of all the tenants right next to our small, airless cubical. When Manning finally roused himself to make coffee, he served himself without offering any to our uninvited guest. The agent, sitting with his pen and notebook poised, announced that he was there to debrief him on his Guatemalan stay—apparently wives were not part of the protocol. Manning responded only that he had nothing to say, and the agent could read his thesis when it was finished.

That was my first encounter with agents who had more (or perhaps less) than a theoretical interest in anthropology. Only then did I begin to realize that our research fit into a larger domain of state intrigue that may even have guided our destiny to Guatemala at that time. Manning's book *Machine Age Maya*, published in 1958, probably had little of interest to the CIA, then or even later. It was, as some called it, a functionalist argument for an existing agreement, extolling the benefits of modernization and industrial production.[5] Although I had contributed field data, maps, interviews, and census materials to the project, I had little to do with the final formulation of the book since I came down with a lingering case of hepatitis B that kept me in the hospital too weak to write or even think for months following our return.

Guatemala was a distant memory in 1962 when I was asked to assist in one of the first training programs for Peace Corps volunteers heading for the western highlands. We began our training in Las Cruces, with course work at New Mexico State University and then a practicum on the Navajo Dulce reservation. The political issues of why the U.S. State Department had chosen Guatemala as a Peace Corps location did not occur to me or to the volunteers, most of whom were just out of college and eager to see the world.

I was interested in seeing what could be done with cooperatives of cultivation and production in rural areas. I returned to Guatemala the following summer in a break from my work in Chiapas to visit one of the cooperatives in which volunteers worked with lay Catholic promoters near Todos Santos. I was impressed with the commitment of the Guatemalans to the producer cooperative and the real income that directly benefited the Indians. This was not growth measured in abstract gross national production, but in daily income that put food into the mouths of children. Much later I read in Burton Hersch's *The Old Boys* (1984) that this cooperative and others being developed at the same time in the area by the Roman Catholic Church and the Peace Corps were considered by the U.S. State Department to be centers of communist subversion. Some were on the target list of the paramilitaries even before José Efraín Ríos Montt came to power (Hersh 1984).

In my thesis fieldwork with Mayas in the Mexican state of Chiapas, I have often reflected on but never written about the differences in state and ethnic relations in the two nations. Both in Chiapas and in Guatemala, relations within communities were crystallized in hierarchical relations based on age and gender, contained within a wider continuum beyond the communities characterized by race and class strata (Adams 1964). In Guatemala after World War II, contact with missionaries of a reinvigorated Catholic Church, agents of the United Nations, the U.S. Peace Corps, and a variety of nongovernmental organizations (NGOs) ignited the sense of injustice among Indians and the fear of rebellion among ladinos. The Mexican Revolution of 1910–17 came late to Chiapas, where the overt racism that governed interactions delayed application of the new rights ethnic minorities had gained in the 1927 constitution. Ladinos retained domination of local communities until the generation of Indians educated in boarding schools in the 1930s came of age in the 1950s. This differed from the rest of Mexico, where elites of the *mestizaje* (mixed races) responded to new revolutionary codes defined by an *indigenista* ideology that extolled the past glories of indigenous civilizations but assumed that the future must necessarily be defined in Western terms.

Chiapas Indians retained their social identity as members of endogamous villages, even though they engaged in trade and traveled to the coastal plantations, where they worked seasonally for ladino and foreign landowners. The first cohort of literate Indians in Chiapas graduated from boarding schools established by Lázaro Cárdenas in the 1930s and 1940s, and by the 1950s they began to occupy town positions of mayor and secretary, which had formerly been occupied by ladinos. During my first field stay in Chiapas in 1957 I saw indigenous participation blossom at the local level, though the politics had not yet become distorted by *caciquismo*—bossism marked by the Party of the Institutional Revolution (Partido Revolucionario Institucional, PRI), which corrupted and divided local leaders from the base.

In Guatemala the relations among Indians, ladinos, and foreign elites were patterned on a colonial model of large landowners and governing caudillos similar to that found in Chiapas. This pattern persisted long after independence from Spain, when the frontier between Mexico and Guatemala was set in 1824. But enormous variation related to the ratios of Indians to ladinos, mode of production, and regional cultural variation reflects a process of ladinization over centuries of contact and assimilation (Adams 1964: 293). Guatemala's revolution of 1944 was a stunning rejection of U.S. support for Jorge Ubico y Castañeda's reinforcement of an agricultural export economy during the 1920s and 1930s, when Mexico had already rejected that model (Torres-Rivas 1991:22). After Ubico was forced to resign during a general strike of students and workers, Juan José Arévalo emerged as the overwhelming winner of the elections that followed. The opening to democracy allowed urban workers, those on commercial agricultural plantations employing more than five thousand, and railroad workers to organize.

While Arévalo concentrated on programs in education, medical care, and housing, his successor to the presidency, Jacobo Arbenz, moved ahead with agrarian reform and major development projects that alarmed the national bourgeois opposition. His aggressive administration of the new land reform legislation ignited further opposition from the United States. During the Eisenhower presidency, when the United States turned its attention from the European theater of war and the postwar reconstruction, John Foster Dulles, who served as secretary of state, and his brother Allen, who was head of the CIA, spearheaded the first major undercover operation to overthrow an elected president in the Western Hemisphere (Cullather 1999).

The destinies of Mayas on either side of the Mexican-Guatemalan border began to diverge following the U.S.-instigated coup in Guatemala after 1954. Whereas the Mexican mestizo elites who directed the course of change after their revolution and up until the 1960s tried to co-opt indigenous groups into their national project, the military leaders who seized power after the Guatemalan coup pursued the militarization instigated by the United States. The nationalistic project in Mexico promoted integration of Indians in accord with a uniform ethnic model, leading to ethnocidal suppression of indigenous languages, customs, and law in public life. In contrast, the export-oriented production dominated by European elites in Guatemala promoted genocidal conflict.

Both ethnocide and genocide are rooted in structural violence, or the everyday deprivation of the basic needs of survival. When structural violence against a subordinate group erupts into a direct attempt to eradicate the cultural characteristics and communal expression of difference, this becomes ethnocide; when this in turn escalates into physical extermination, it becomes genocide. Both expressions are condemned by U.N. covenants, but it is extremely difficult to pin the label of genocide on any group; for example, rampant killing of whole communities in Darfur proceeded for decades before the term *genocide* was even mentioned in U.N. circles. This is because the term implies that the world community should take action against the aggressors.

At the most general level, the reason for the difference in the course of ethnocide and genocide can be traced to the level of development of civil society. Mexico had developed civil society networks that linked pueblos, which then were drawn into wider circuits promoted by the postrevolutionary project of forging a nation. Yet the *indigenista* ideology underlying the PRI undercut the basis for an authentic indigenous society while extolling the Indian past. As Miguel Bartolomé (1994: 73) demonstrates in his analysis of three cultures coexisting in the Mexican state of Oaxaca, the state maintains a pluralistic discourse at the formal level, but an internalization of ethnic inequality in practice. The eradication of indigenous languages, he maintains, is part of a broader policy of ethnocide pursued in state educational and economic policies that strive toward homogeneity (Bartolomé 1994: 74–75).

The ethnocidal practices that characterize Chiapas policies of integration contrast with the Guatemalan experience following the 1954 U.S.-engineered coup. Whereas civilian leaders guided the popular mandates of indigenous and mestizo peoples in Mexico, Guatemala was ruled directly, and with only brief civilian interludes indirectly, by the military in communication with U.S. special forces. The genocidal policies resulted in the decimation of over 200,000 indigenous people over the course of a thirty-six-year armed conflict.

Following the 1954 coup, the Guatemalan military leaders chose—or were pressed into adopting—military strategies to eliminate every form of participatory activity, from factory workers' unions such as those in Cantel, to rural campesino producers and sellers organizations. Civil society had grown enormously in the decade of liberty offered by the democratic governments of Arévalo and Arbenz. The General Confederation of Guatemalan Workers (Confederación General de Trabajadores Guatemaltecos, CGTG) had 90,000 members, the National Peasant Confederation of Guatemala (Confederación Nacional Campesina de Guatemala, CNCG) was expanding branches in the countryside, and political parties were developing new positions (ODHAG 1999: 185).

Arbenz's promotion of agrarian reform prompted a reaction that resounded from the banana plantation of United Fruit to its headquarters in Boston and to Washington, where the politically powerful Dulles brothers held large investments in the company. When Arbenz realized that the army refused to fight and that there were insufficient arms for the volunteers from the Guatemalan confederations of workers and peasants, he renounced his post; that was the evening of June 27, 1954 (CEH 1999, 1:105–107; Handy 1994: 189–190). Shortly thereafter, Castillo Armas was seated as president, and the makeshift government succeeded in bringing about the reversal of the democratic process. The stark racism of the ruling elites fueled by the anticommunist agenda of the U.S. State Department grew with each attack on the indigenous populations. In the first two months of the regime change, Castillo Armas proceeded with his project of liquidating the revolution by forcibly dislocating a hundred thousand peasants from the land they legally owned and worked (Torres Rivas 1991:8). Uncounted numbers died from starvation when the former owners of the lands that had been donated during the revolution drove their cattle into the fields to destroy the crops the peasants had planted. Castillo Armas was responsible not only for commanding this operation, but for commandeering the corn imported at low prices from Mexico and selling it for personal profit in the Guatemalan market. The military uprising against José Miguel Ydígoras Fuentes in 1960 resulted in the retreat of dissidents to the mountains and in the formation of guerrilla insurgency in 1962.

The United States took advantage of violent shifts of power in subsequent years to intensify military interventions in Guatemala. The Green Berets who had fought in Vietnam helped direct counterinsurgency campaigns financed by the U.S. Army and led by Colonel Carlos Arana Osorio from 1966 to 1968 (Perera 1993: 41). The harsh attack on Guatemalan indigenous communities escalated from 1974 to 1985. The terror began in 1978 with the Panzós massacre in Alta Verapaz. This was not an area of guerrilla activity, such as the plantation area to the east, where former plantation owners (many of them German who were the first to be affected by land reform) were dislocating Indians who had received land grants under the Arbenz government. The highly publicized massacre occurred when settlers tried to defend their lands against the oil companies that were expanding their drilling into the settled areas of the Ixcán. The army and paramilitary forces backed up the companies against the settlers, who objected to the takeover of the lands they had cleared and settled (Falla 1994, Sinclair 1995: 85). It came to be called the Zone of the Generals, since it was the site where General Lucas and other army generals grabbed land in areas where transnational U.S. oil explorers, including Getty Oil, Texaco, Amoco, and Shenandoah Oil, had discovered oil (Jonas 1991: 128, Sinclair 1995: 85). Labor unrest of striking workers in 1975 in the Coca-Cola factory and in the mines in 1977 marked the increase in protest and rebellion that culminated in the formation of the Committee for Peasant Unity (Comité de Unidad Campesina, CUC), a community action organization of indigenes and mestizos, in 1978. The government retaliated ever more forcefully, violating international accords with the 1980 attack on Maya peasant organizations that occupied the Spanish embassy to protest military massacres.

The peak of armed hostilities occurred from 1982 to 1983, when General Ríos Montt carried out a reign of terror leading to the killing of over 10,000 Mayas and forcing into exile over 100,000 rural villagers. In the subsequent militarization of the entire society, indigenous youths were forced to join patrols in search of dissidents. Their complicity, driven by fear for their lives, reinforced the militarization of the society. Some, however, resisted by joining the CUC, others joined the Guerrilla Army of the Poor (Ejército Guerrillero de los Pobres, EGP), especially after the massacre in Rio Negro in 1982, when the Guatemalan army killed over half the villagers because they opposed the damming of a river for an international hydroelectric company (Alecio 1995: 26). However, the unleashing of state terror failed to eradicate their identity as indigenous people (Green 1999).

In the wake of the bloody slaughter, Guatemalan elites fostered an export-oriented economy that recorded increases in gross national product benefiting a narrow foreign investment sector with few gains from an increasingly impoverished working class. The experience of the Glamis Gold Marlin Mining project in San Miguel Ixtahuacán in 2005 presaged what happened when the Central American Free Trade Agreement (CAFTA) officially went into effect in 2009, curtailing national restraints on foreign corporations. Mam leaders say they were tricked into signing a contract for development with Marlin Corporation that surrendered property rights for operating a mine on land they considered inalienable. Massive demonstrations protesting the operation of the mine resulted in one death in March 2005 (Henderson 2005).

In Mexico the break from PRI hegemony over indigenous municipalities began with the mobilization for the 1974 National Indigenous Forum (Foro Nacional Indígena) and peaked with the 1992 quincentennial-strengthened civil society. This break from decades of PRI control prepared them for the greater struggle for indigenous autonomy when the Salinas policies of neoliberal development resulted in the 1992 "reform" of the Agrarian Reform Law allowing privatization of the *ejido*—communal lands distributed by the agrarian reform—and the signing of the North American Free Trade Agreement. It fueled support for the Zapatista Army for National Liberation (Ejército Zapatista de Liberación Nacional, EZLN) that had been training for ten years prior to the 1994 uprising in the Lacandón uprising.

Comparing the indigenous state relations in Guatemala and Chiapas, it is clear that U.S. intervention has promoted more flagrant genocidal policies affecting Mayas in Guatemala than in Mexico. Even though the Mexican government has verged on genocide to oppose the Zapatista uprising, military and paramilitary attacks have repeatedly been thwarted by civil society (J. Nash 2001). Since Guatemala's ladino population with a narrow European constituency constitutes a minority of the national population, terrorist policies exercised by the state following the coup have rarely been confronted by the massive civil society demonstrations that are seen in Mexico.

Back to the Center of the World

This state practice has played out in the local site I worked in since the coup. Not until 1985 did I revisit Cantel, nineteen years after the civil war had begun and eleven years before it was officially declared over (Jonas 2004). Santiago Xitimul was in a wheelchair after a stroke. After he was mayor, he had joined the army in the 1960s. He spoke only briefly and with difficulty of his being recruited by the Guatemalan army and receiving training in the U.S. Department of Defense School of the Americas (now called the Western Hemisphere Institute for Security Cooperation) at Fort Benning, Georgia. Since I knew him as a decent man with modest ambitions, it alarmed me to realize how far militarization had penetrated the Guatemalan countryside. I did not question him about the war years, nor did I ask him whether there was a massacre in Cantel. Subconsciously I did not want to know what he might have done in the name of anticommunism, nor did I want him to reveal events that might implicate him. I also learned that Cruz Ixcot, who had been my main informant for my study of Protestant conversion (1960), was still tending his grain mill and led the Presbyterian congregation he had formed.

I interviewed the plant manager, who told me that the Cantel Fábrica de Textiles had replaced the 1895 weaving machines from England that were in use when we lived in Cantel in 1954. Since the new machines required less labor-intensive work, many more men than women now constituted the workforce, since they occupied engineering and maintenance positions. Our close friends, the family of Juan Quiem, who worked in the factory, were all alive and well, though Juan had retired from the factory to work in his milpa. The little girls who used to carry water jugs, carefully calibrated to their size and strength, from the fountain in the plaza to their home, were now grown up and had families of their own. Juan recalled the party that he and his wife Roberta hosted on the twelfth day of Christmas, when they celebrated the recovery of the baby Jesús from his compadre's house in the factory compound. I remembered with nostalgia the procession of a hundred or more guests carrying candles up the 500-foot rise to the pueblo in what seemed a constant stream of light.

We did not speak of the violence and terror that had visited the highlands in the interim. I felt that it would be weeks before they or I could talk with confidence about the changes they had experienced. While I was in Guatemala City I read each day of bodies found by the police with no indication of how they had been killed. Guatemala was still living the nightmare unleashed by the coup, and over 200,000 had fled across the Mexican border into Chiapas. Much as I had hoped to return to Guatemala to do more fieldwork, I could not bring students into such a dangerous and threatening environment. Instead, I chose to return to my old field station in Chiapas. That was the beginning of my interest in comparing Mayas across the national border of Guatemala and Mexico.

Witnessing in Guatemala, a New Ethnological Role

I returned to Guatemala in September 2002 as part of a delegation to attend the trial of high-ranking Guatemalan military officials for allegedly ordering the murder in 1990 of Myrna Mack, a Guatemalan anthropologist who was doing research on military atrocities at a time when few dared even to mention the deeds. The court judgment against one of the three officers charged with the crime marked the first conviction of a high military leader for violations committed during the country's undeclared armed conflict (Washington Post 2002: A23).

We were charged with visiting NGOs responsible for reporting criminal acts and thus ending impunity for the military. Our activities included visits with the Association for the Advance of Social Sciences in Guatemala (Asociación para el Avance de las Ciencias Sociales, AVANCSO), a social-anthropology research team founded by Myrna Mack that works with survivors in the villages that had suffered massacres, and with two forensic teams, the Center for Forensic Analysis and Applied Sciences (Centro de Análisis Forense y Ciencias Aplicadas, CAFCA) and the Guatemalan Forensic Anthropology Foundation (Fundación de Antropología Forense de Guatemala, FAFG). We also met with representatives of the Guatemalan National Coalition for Human Rights (Comisión Nacional de los Derechos Humanos de Guatemala, CNDHG) and the National Coordinating Committee for Campesino Organizations (Coordinadora Nacional de Organizaciones Campesinas, CNOC).

We learned during our week with these organizations the value of team work and sharing information among the physical and social-anthropology teams. Working with survivors of the massacres, social anthropologists recovered the historical memories of those who witnessed the atrocities. Exhuming the remains of the victims from makeshift burial sites, forensic teams retrieved the buried history contained in the bones of the murdered. We also learned to appreciate the extraordinary courage exhibited by investigators and the danger to the fledgling democracy still posed by clandestine paramilitary organizations. When the forensic research teams discovered that indigenous informants turned away when they saw national guards sent by the police in response to reported threats, they decided to work without protection. They worked closely with the social anthropologists and realized how important the narratives were to identifying the skeletal remains. Together, the physical and social anthropologists filled in gaps in the historical record caused by the repression and violence exercised against indigenous people over the past thirty-six years.

Poignant reminders of the current danger emerged throughout our visit. On September 5, 2002, just three days before we arrived, the CAFCA forensic team received a letter containing abusive language, warning that "we are not going to let your work get published," and threatening that there might be a bomb on Wednesday or Thursday. (The academic maxim "Publish or perish" is reconfigured in times of stress.) Some paid the penalty: on September 6, the body of one of the assistants to the forensic anthropologists was found with his eyes gouged out, his tongue wrenched from his throat, and his ears ripped off.

We were physically overwhelmed with the horror of past events when we stepped through the courtyard of the FAFG and saw it filled with child-size coffins containing remains from the exhumation site. The attending policeman held our identification documents and watched us with a scrutinizing eye while we interviewed the staff. The director, José Suasnavar, told us, "We are working more than before. In our case, threats continue and we do not know the source since we have done so many investigations. More and more people are getting interested. Most of those who seek information are young people from twenty to twenty-five years of age. In the early days, few people came to us because of fear. Repeated information reinforces the desire of the people to know what happened to family members and neighbors. But we are increasingly attacked with threats."

Clara Arenas, director of the offices of AVANCSO, recounted the threats and assaults endured by social anthropologists as they carried out fieldwork in highland indigenous communities under the military terror, which had increased between 2001 and 2002. Matilde González, who with a team of AVANSCO researchers was eliciting memories of the terror, was followed and accosted in January 2002 by an unidentified man, and the research center was burglarized, with disks and computers holding data stolen or vandalized. "We have to break the authoritarian culture," Clara Arenas asserted. She and other members of the team see their task as investigators as that of informing society how the hegemonic base of the military and state operated at the grassroots, inculcating its authoritarian practices in village society through civilian patrols so as to disintegrate the social fabric. The very success of their work in analyzing the military tentacles in this social context appeared to be the reason for the mounting threats in 2002.

In the process of our investigations of what the Guatemalan attorney general's office and the human rights office were doing about the threats, our initial insistence that the center should have increased security and surveillance now seemed absurd to us. Our very presence in the country on this mission might well have garnered more danger for our colleagues and the government officials working against such insurmountable odds. And we would not be there to take the same risks that they bore of retaliation from the still-active *guardias blancas*—white guards, or paramilitaries. But as I watched the proceedings of the trial of the officers in a courtroom where some of the survivors of the massacres they triggered were in the audience, I was overwhelmed with certainty about the need for this performance and the research process that provided the necessary evidence for the conviction. The recourse to judicial processes may, as some critics claim, fall into the trap of yet another neoliberal showpiece, but it can evoke consciousness of the social rejection of violations that exceed basic human conditions.[6]

Reconciliation and Redemption

My next and most recent trip to Guatemala was in March 2005, when I carried out research into development that had occurred since the 1950s (J. Nash 2008). When I visited Cantel, the town offices were bustling with people. I told the clerk that I wanted to talk of changes in the town since I lived there in 1953, and he referred me to a young man, Ramón Riqucheq, an ecologist in charge of environmental conservation. He quickly sketched in the major changes: Each pueblo has control of water and wood resources. Few agriculturalists remained where once even the textile factory workers planted the two hectares lent to them by the owners. Employment was down, with over 3,500 jobs eliminated a few years earlier when Japanese and Asian competition forced local manufacturers nearly into bankruptcy. The only active factory is a small artisan shop employing forty-nine workers blowing glass sold on the world market. Women who were *viudas* (widows)—either because their husbands died or had migrated to the United States or Canada to work—wove shawls with material supplied by a cooperative started by a German woman. Women also assembled garments in their own homes if they had machines, or in other houses where they were employed at less than the minimum wage. There were no *maquilas* (factories) in town.

Ramón Riquechek saw as the major problem the growth of an illegal economy with corruption in high places in government. He attributed the high unemployment to overpopulation: people continued to have many children, although there were family planning clinics assisted by a German funding agency. There were fifty-four midwives and two health stations. Whereas there was no fire or ambulance service in 1954, the town now had both these public services. President Óscar Berger Perdomo (who left office in 2008) had been more effective than his predecessors in bringing municipal services, such as the environmental conservation service.

Although I did not mention the war years, Ramón volunteered the information that Cantel suffered many attacks on its people when Fernando Romeo Lucas García and Ríos Montt occupied the presidency. He felt that Cantel was targeted as a Zona Roja (red zone) because of the union, commenting that many were killed without reason by the *escuadrones de muerte* (death squads) and defense patrols assigned to the town. In 2002, however, according to Ramón the town had "coordinated programs with three Peace Corps volunteers from the United States working with the women's [weaving] group, another with environmental education, and another with agriculture developing solid waste compost."

In contrast to the readily volunteered information from the conservation agent, I learned little in my interview with the manager of the Cantel Fábrica de Textiles. A graduate in economics from the Universidad de San Carlos, he commented on the scarcity of opportunities for many graduates from Guatemalan colleges and universities. He claimed that, with the recent purchase of high-efficiency machines, factory production was at the same level with 350 employees as it had been with ten times that number. It was hard for me to reconcile that claim with what some municipal officers said about the factory being close to bankruptcy. The wage averaged "a little above the minimum wage" he said, and when I asked what that was, he denied knowledge of the figure.

I later learned from people in the town center of Cantel that the minimum wage is 40 quetzales (about $6 U.S.) a day and that unemployment was high. The municipio of Cantel was reduced to sending its youths to the United States or Canada to work, relying on funds they were able to send back to Cantel. Juan Quiem had eight grandchildren working in New York State and the southeastern United States. All were undocumented migrants and lived in fear of being expelled.

Yet despite the fact that the town was suffering the trauma of years of militarization, there were signs of progress. Joaquín Pablo Salas, who came to Cantel in 1995, is director of the health clinic that he built in 2000 with money and land donated by the town, and the town has an ambulance that connects patients with Quetzaltenango. Salas was forthcoming about the deficiencies as well as the advances that have come forth. His specialty is preventive medicine, promoting educational programs to improve sanitation, nutrition, and water treatment that are disseminated by radio and seminars held in town, as well as volunteers who visit rural hamlets. He spoke freely about continuing violence, although it is not as extreme as in 1982. Much of it is internalized violence, and he enumerated suicides, domestic abuse, and alcoholism. *Maras* and *pandillas* (youth gangs) still generate public violence, defiling public properties and carrying out assassinations.

The structural violence resulting from poverty shows up in sicknesses resulting from lack of hygiene and exposure to contaminated environments. Tuberculosis is not as common as it was, but AIDS has come to Cantel; also, because people no longer have land on which to grow food, childhood developmental problems related to poorer nutrition are beginning to appear. Prepared foods and especially bottled soft drinks use up already-scarce income but provide little or no nutritional benefit to children. Even more disturbing are fetal abnormalities that midwives are reporting to the clinic. Salas has seen fetuses with no more formation than "a bunch of grapes for the head" born to women in Pasac, an *aldea* (small village) where midwives have also delivered babies with holes in their spines. "We are administering folic acid to overcome poor maternal diet," Salas said, "but that is not always effective," attributing some of these developmental problems to contamination of the environment. He deplores the use of pesticides in surrounding towns such as Almolonga and Salcajá, which are engaged in vegetable and fruit production. The water irrigating these commercial crops drains into the Samalá River, which carries the pesticides and fertilizers downstream.

The quest for a democratic, fiscally responsible, and just government is in a fragile balance. People with whom I spoke in 2006 reiterated the following complaints about what is happening in the Guatemalan government:

1. Corruption in government from the federal to the local level. New officials who have arrived with President Berger fall into the practices of their predecessors, preferring to carry out projects "without seals," that is without official, signed documents of procurement.
2. The military still has budgetary priority to carry out "modernizing" projects with ill-defined financial input. Generals receive pensions of 10,000 quetzales a month, while most public servants receive little or

no pension. Many former soldiers have joined pandillas that rob and vandalize public and private property.

3. Pandillas operate with impunity. Some people guess they are ordered by those who are trying to discredit civilian governmental operations, vandalizing property as they did in Cantel when the medical station was inaugurated. They distract people's attention from the real and present danger of another military takeover of the government.

4. There is inadequate coordination among religious, governmental, and NGO activists, some of whom seem guided more by the desire to enhance the prestige of their organizations than to respond to the needs of the people.

5. An inadequate penal and justice system releases convicted felons from jail and continue with corrupt processes. Former President Alfonso Portillo Cabrera has been accused of absconding with $500 million U.S., but people expect he will go free.

Conclusions

I write this as Guatemala is entering another dramatic cycle, with democratic forces reconnoitering as militarized gangs are attempting to regain power in this war-torn country. The Bush agenda to contain the rising rebellions in Latin America against neoliberal trade policies was rejected in the 2008 presidential election, raising hope that President Barack Obama will forestall further attempts to intervene in the internal politics of the region. This may provide a breathing space for the Guatemalan government to overcome a history of violence with impunity. The heroic efforts of social science and forensic research teams, and of human rights activists within and beyond the borders of Guatemala, may prevail.

Anthropologists can no longer ignore the global conflicts in which we become immersed in the course of our fieldwork. We went into field situations innocent of these plots spawned in the emergent empire of post–World War II and the role that we might unconsciously play. Now too much is known about the undercover plots of secret agents and special forces—first in Iran in 1953 when the CIA engineered the overthrow of Mosaddegh, and then with the overthrow of Jacobo Arbenz in Guatemala in 1954—to ignore or deny U.S. intervention in the field sites we choose. Other covert operations fomented during the cold war installed military dictators in Bolivia and Brazil in 1964. With the advice of U.S. National Security Advisor Henry Kissinger,

President Richard Nixon engineered the overthrow of the democratically elected Chilean president, Salvador Allende, on September 11 in 1973. Over a decade later Reagan defended his destabilization of Central American countries, now including El Salvador and Nicaragua, as well as intensifying counterinsurgency in Guatemala. Oliver North took the blame for payoffs made to mercenary Honduran contras or rebel troops in carrying out the "dirty wars" that ravaged these countries in the 1980s.

We have to ask ourselves what role we play in setting the conditions that lead to military regimes and the destruction of democracy in the areas we study. Who is going to benefit by what we publish, and who might be compromised by our interpretations? What role can we play as activists, both to reveal what we learned about past errors, and to try to bring about a change in direction? We can no longer affect the naïveté of the anthropologist as hero, as Claude Lévi-Straus once called the anthropologist embarking on adventures into the unknown. We are on the other side of the looking glass, where the dark image we cast is reflected in the eyes of those who observe us. In this new role we can only find acceptance as collaborators with those we study, as we share with them knowledge of our culture as we discover theirs.

Notes

A version of this chapter was published in June C. Nash, *Practicing Ethnography in a Globalizing World: An Anthropological Odyssey* (Lanham, Md.: AltaMira Press, 2007).

1. At a time when the field of social anthropology was focused on the functioning of colonized societies and the structural imperatives for maintaining them, Gluckman voiced a strong critique of segregationist apartheid policies in South Africa and noted the importance of social conflict (Gluckman 1940). In Gluckman 1964 he suggests the need to overcome the prevailing limitations in the field that his students sought to overcome (Kapferer 2006).

2. I have borrowed the title of Paule Marshall's book, *The Chosen Place, the Timeless People,* which captures the naïveté of anthropologists working in her native Barbados, to highlight the naive assumptions we held in the 1950s with our treatment of the world as a laboratory.

3. This would later be confirmed since after the coup he was known to have acted as an informant to the factory management and helped round up union instigators who were imprisoned on the assumption that they were communists.

4. Throughout this entire time during our fieldwork, we *never* saw any campesinos with arms. Moreover, a stringer for the *New York Times* living in Guatemala confirmed to us that the arms were never delivered.

5. See, for example, Manning Nash (1960).

6. Shannon Speed (2005) has summarized the arguments of scholars who are studying human rights defenders, showing how the specious use of the discourse of human rights may undermine the process of achieving the rights.

Works Cited

Adams, Richard N.
  1964   Encuesta sobre la cultura de los ladinos en Guatemala. 2nd edition. Gua-
          temala: Seminario de Integración Social Guatemalteca, Centro Editorial
          José de Pineda Ibarra, Ministerio de Educación Público.

Alecio, Rolando
  1995   Uncovering the Truth: Political Violence and Indigenous Organizations. *In*
          The New Politics of Survival: Grassroots Movements in Central America.
          Minor Sinclair, ed. Pp. 25–46. New York: Monthly Review Press.

Bartolomé, Miguel Alberto
  1994   La represión de la pluralidad y los derechos indígenas en Oaxaca. *In*
          Derechos Indígenas en la Actualidad. Pp. 73–99. México: IIJ-UNAM.

CEH (Comisión para el Eslaracimiento Histórico)
  1999   Guatemala memoria del silencio. Informe para el esclarecimiento histórico.
          Guatemala: CEH.

Cullather, Nick
  1999   Secret History: The CIA's Classified Account of the Operations in Guate-
          mala, 1952–1954. Palo Alta, Calif.: Stanford University Press.

Falla, Ricardo
  1978   Quiché rebelde. Guatemala: Editorial Universitaria de Guatemala.
  1994   Massacres in the Jungle: Ixcán, Guatemala 1974–1982. Julia Howland, trans.
          Boulder, Colo.: Westview Press.

Gluckman, Max
  1940   Analysis of Social Situation in Modern Zululand. Bantu Studies 14:1–30.
  1964   Closed Systems and Open Minds: The Limits of Naïveté in Social Anthro-
          pology. Chicago: Aldine Press (reprinted 2007).

Green, Linda
  1999   Fear as a Way of Life: Maya Women in Rural Guatemala. New York: Co-
          lumbia University Press.

Handy, Jim
  1994   Revolution in the Countryside: Rural Conflict and Agrarian Reform. Chapel
          Hill: University of North Carolina Press.

Henderson, Kathryn
  2005   Murder Linked to Marlin Mine Workers in Guatemala. Cultural Survival.
          culturalsurvival.org, accessed March 25, 2009.

Hersh, Burton
  1992   The Old Boys: The American Elite and the Origins of the CIA. New York: Charles Scribner's.
Hutchinson, R. C.
  1949   Elephant and Castle: A Reconstruction. New York: Rinehart.
Jonas, Susanne
  1991   The Battle for Guatemala: Rebels, Death Squads, and U.S. Power. Boulder, Colo.: Westview Press.
  2004   "The Lessons from Guatemala." Unpublished manuscript.
Kapferer, Bruce
  2006   Situations, Crisis, and the Anthropology of the Concrete. In The Manchester School: Practice and Ethnographic Praxis in Anthropology. T. M. S. Evans and Don Handelman, eds. Pp. 188–135. Oxford and New York: Berghahn Books.
Nash, June
  1960   Protestantism in an Indian Village in the Western Highlands of Guatemala. Alpha Kappa Deltan Quarterly (Claremont College, Calif.): 49–53.
  2001   Mayan Visions: The Quest for Autonomy in an Age of Globalization. New York: Routledge.
  2008   Development to Unite Us: Autonomy and Multicultural Coexistence in Chiapas and Guatemala. New Proposals: Journal of Marxism and Interdisciplinary Inquiry 1(1):14–39.
Nash, Manning
  1958   Machine Age Maya: The Industrialization of a Guatemalan Community. University of Chicago Press. Memoirs of the American Anthropology Association 87.
ODHAG (Oficina de Derechos Humanos del Arzobispado de Guatemala)
  1999   Guatemala: Never Again! The Official Report of the Recovery of Historical Memory Project (REMHI), Human Rights Office, Archdiocese of Guatemala. Maryknoll, N.Y.: Orbis Books.
Perera, Victor
  1993   Unfinished Conquest: The Guatemalan Tragedy. Berkeley: University of California Press.
Sinclair, Minor
  1995   Faith, Community and Resistance in the Guatemalan Highlands. In The New Politics of Survival: Grassroots Movements in Central America. Minor Sinclair, ed. Pp. 75–108. New York: Monthly Review Press.
Speed, Shannon
  2005   Dangerous Discourses: Human Rights and Multiculturalism in Neoliberal Mexico. PoLAR: Political and Legal Anthropology Review 28(1):29–51.

Torres Rivas, Edelberto

1991   Presentation by the Prosecutor. *In* Guatemala: Tyranny on Trial: Testimony of the Permanent People's Tribunal. Susanne Jonas, Ed McCaughan, and Elizabeth Sutherland Martínez, eds. Pp. 7–23. San Francisco: Synthesis Publications.

Washington Post

Guatemalan Ex-Officer Is Convicted of Murder; Military Critic Slain during Civil War. October 4, 2002: A23.

3

A Democracy Born in Violence

Maya Perceptions of the 1944 Patzicía Massacre and the 1954 Coup

DAVID CAREY JR.

What is striking about the events of 1954 in Maya-Kaqchikel (henceforth Kaqchikel) popular memory is their obscurity in Kaqchikel reconstructions of the past. Seldom do Colonel Carlos Castillo Armas's (1954–57) overthrow of Colonel Jacobo Arbenz Guzmán (1951–54) and the role of the U.S. Central Intelligence Agency (CIA) emerge in Kaqchikel oral histories. This elision is even more pronounced in women's historical narratives. Though oral tradition is a significant repository for Kaqchikel formulations and revisions of the past, other sources such as clothing and topography serve as mnemonic devices of history. Similarly, a mural painted on the cemetery walls of San Juan Comalapa (henceforth Comalapa) in 2002 provides a glimpse into how and why Kaqchikels remember the past. The sixty-one-panel display begins with idyllic scenes of the pre-Hispanic era and culminates with the signing of the Peace Accords in 1996 and the hope of building a more peaceful, egalitarian, and fruitful society. Much like in oral narratives, the 1976 earthquake that leveled much of the central highlands and the civil war (1960–96) that claimed over 200,000 lives command considerable attention in these images; in fact, the former flows into the latter as if to indicate a causal relationship. The absence of the state in general and reference to the political machinations and reverberations of 1954 in particular is noteworthy in this expression of Kaqchikel history. If scholars have identified the 1954 coup as a watershed in Guatemala's history, why do so many Mayas fail to emphasize it? How would the chapters in this book be received in Guatemala, not just among ladino and Maya intellectuals but particularly among rural Mayas? Would most Mayas agree, "Guatemala's society and current history *must be* read through the lens of 1954–55?" What historical junctures figure prominently in their reformulations of their lived experience? How do Maya perceptions of the state affect their historical perspectives? And how does gender affect the ways Mayas experience, remember, and think about the state?

Examining Maya perceptions of national events demonstrates the articulation between national and local forces. Kaqchikels thought a great deal about the state, but for the most part they did not think much of it. For those who experienced the state as capricious and reckless, it was better to be ruled by a harsh yet predictable caudillo. If they conformed to his rule, they could pursue their goals within the established parameters; they knew who to consult to achieve their goals. According to Kaqchikel elders, community leaders periodically enjoyed an audience with one such dictator: General Jorge Ubico y Castañeda (1931–44). And he often addressed their concerns and needs expeditiously. Yet even when individual leaders like Ubico were ruling with an iron fist, it was difficult for the state to institutionalize mechanisms of control down to the local level. So penetration of the state into Maya communities was limited. Often *cofradías* (religious brotherhoods) and *municipalidades indígenas* (indigenous municipalities) deflected the advances of the state (Esquit 1996: 63, 2002: 148–156). Of course, they also largely blocked women's access to power and resources. Local state officials, such as *intendentes* during the Ubico regime, often had little understanding of how Maya institutions operated. If they had, authorities probably would have seen such organizations as subversive (Gillin 1958).

For their part, Kaqchikel historical narratives reveal that Kaqchikels clearly distinguished between local oppressors and the state. As Carol Smith and others have argued, ladinos often became agents of the state (Smith 1990: 86–87).[1] Yet this alliance was strongest during times when the state was fragile, not when it was powerful. The local ladino racism that pervaded Guatemala was the proxy of a weak state, not the ally of a strong state. Ladinos from Zaragoza who massacred Kaqchikels in 1944 were not agents of the state, but rather were acting on their own behalf at a time when the government was in disarray. The 1944 Patzicía massacre is evidence of the disjunction between local ladinos and the state; the latter did not control the former. And for many Kaqchikels looking back on the 1944 democratic transition, this made the new government dangerous.

In Guatemala, the state contributed to the failure of its hegemonic project. With few exceptions, Kaqchikel oral histories depict Guatemala's government to be morally bankrupt, ideologically racist, and fundamentally exploitative. These perceptions emboldened Kaqchikel confidence in their own views of

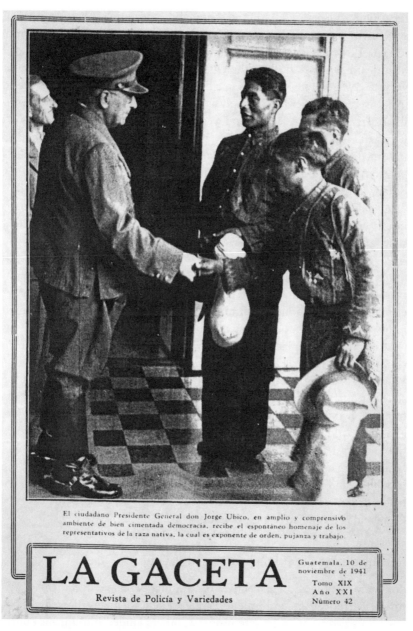

El ciudadano Presidente General don Jorge Ubico, en amplio y comprensivo ambiente de bien cimentada democracia, recibe el espontáneo homenaje de los representativos de la raza nativa, la cual es exponente de orden, pujanza y trabajo.

LA GACETA

Revista de Policía y Variedades

Guatemala, 10 de
noviembre de 1941
Tomo XIX
Año XXI
Número 42

President General Jorge Ubico meeting with "representatives of the *raza nativa*."
(*Gaceta de Policía*, Nov. 10, 1941)

the nation, which rejected cultural assimilation and at times Western political systems, including democracy. With the notable exception of the Ubico and, to a lesser extent, General Justo Rufino Barrios (1873–85) regimes, Kaqchikel historical narratives portray the Guatemalan government as dangerously wanton (Warren 1989: 61).[2] When citizens consider the state evil, they tend to flee or resist, rather than comply as the state would wish. For survivors of the Patzicía massacre, ladinos too were evil. A long history of nefarious officials and their deleterious policies, actions, and presence in the highlands informed Kaqchikel perceptions of ladinos and the state. When Kaqchikels perceived the state and its representatives as heedless, alien, and unjust, they distanced themselves from the national political and social agenda, and in turn gained confidence in their own local alternative political forms, identities, and strategies. To inform their dissent, they contrasted a malevolent state (and in some cases ladinos) with honorable Mayas.

For Kaqchikels looking back on the past, the events surrounding the death of the dictatorship and birth of democracy are far more critical historical markers than the CIA-engineered overthrow of Guatemala's democratic government in 1954. Though committed to the ideals of equality and human rights, the democratic government had little understanding of its indigenous citizens. When it replaced a dictator with whom Mayas had established a working relationship, many Mayas were further marginalized. Under Ubico, Kaqchikels had confidence in their place in the nation and a sense that the state periodically responded to their demands. Many feared the democratic transition would take away what they had worked so hard to create (Sanders 2004: 31). And for many, their fears were justified. In this way, the Patzicía massacre cast a shadow over the new government. With the advantage of hindsight, many elders argued the 1954 coup was an inevitable result of the instability and insecurity caused by their nation's transition to democracy before its population was ready for it. Viewed in this way, 1944 better explains Guatemala's recent tragic past than does 1954.

Reconsidering the Primacy of the 1954 Coup

The few accounts and perspectives of 1954 that percolate in Kaqchikel historical narratives are ambivalent. While some Kaqchikels discredited Arbenz for expropriating private property, others lauded him for his efforts to redistribute land to Mayas. Yet often even the latter criticized Arbenz for weakening the nation and then not adequately defending its sovereignty in a time of crisis (Junlajuj K'at, July 9, 1998, Comalapa; Carey Jr. 2001: 259).[3]

Some accused Arbenz of being a communist while others recognized the political motivations behind attaching such a label to him. "The problem was not that Arbenz was a communist, but that he took the land from the banana companies and he enraged the U.S.," noted Oxlajuj Kawoq, a teacher and university student from the Kaqchikel town of San José Poaquil (henceforth Poaquil; March 18, 1998). Many were painfully aware of the role of the United States, United Fruit Company, and CIA played in the coup. Lajuj Kame, an evangelical storeowner in neighboring Comalapa explained:

> Arbenz passed the 900 decree to give land to the people. He was a military colonel who wanted to help the indigenous people, farmers . . . [and] work-ers. He was a humanitarian, but the U.S. did not like that, so they removed him. It pains me that a great nation such as the United States did not want to help a humanitarian. The United Fruit Company . . . supported the invasion of Castillo Armas. Also the U.S. ambassador to Guatemala was [Allen] Foster Dulles, and his brother John Foster Dulles was the secretary of state. So the U.S. looked for a caudillo and it was [Castillo] Armas. . . . The United States terminated Arbenz and that pains me. [Castillo] Armas was killed because he . . . was a traitor. (February 14, 1998)[4]

Ixtijax, a weaver and teacher of the Kaqchikel language, said, "If he had not helped *qawinäq* [our people], he would have finished his term" (August 5, 1998, Comalapa). Though some lamented that Arbenz's overthrow precipi-tated the civil war, most did not draw a causal relationship between the two, in part because they saw them both as part of a larger historical pattern in Guatemala (Lajuj K'at, April 11, 1998, Comalapa; Lajuj Ajpu,' April 19, 1998, Poaquil; B'eleje' Kawoq, June 9, 1998, Tecpán; Ixtojil, February 7, 1998, Ba-rahona; Ka'i' K'at, May 16, 1998, Comalapa; Lajuj Kan, October 16, 1998, Pachitur, Comalapa).

A focus on the civil war that ensued after 1954 often overshadows the violence prior to 1954 and particularly the violence from which Guatemala's democracy was born. One massacre in particular caught the nation's attention as a warning: the 1944 Patzicía massacre. "*Nuwinäq* [my people] do not talk about Arbenz much except for his land reform and that they no longer had to work on the *fincas* [large landed estates], that was good. But the politics is not as important. The Patzicía massacre was more important than the 1954 coup. . . . They associate Patzicía with being afraid of the state [because it] helped ladinos," noted Lajuj K'at, a Kaqchikel intellectual (Comalapa, April 4, 2005). Guatemala's civil war and its escalation to genocide in the early 1980s was undoubtedly a horrifying experience for Mayas, but perhaps they were not as shocked by it as foreign observers were. At best, the infrequent efforts by the state to protect indigenous rights were invariably marked by assimilationist pressures, but often the state undermined Mayas' livelihood, dignity, and their very existence. The long history of injustice that preceded 1954 informed their experience of the last half of the twentieth century. Even Kaqchikels who do not associate the revolutionary junta or Dr. Juan José Arévalo Bermejo (1945–51) with the massacre of hundreds of Kaqchikels in Patzicía fault the state for its inability to prevent it. By questioning the state's legitimacy, their historical narratives of the 1944 Patzicía massacre help to explain why some Mayas could have supported Ubico in the past: Alfonso Antonio Portillo Cabrera (2000–2004) in the 1999 presidential elections, and more alarmingly General José Efraín Ríos Montt after he presided over genocide from 1982 to 1983.

Of course, local circumstances influence such historical and contemporary perspectives of leaders and the state. The impact of the 1944 revolution and the 1954 coup varied from one community to the next. To cite one example, the transition from dictatorship to democracy was almost imperceptible in the Q'eqchi' town of Carchá, where the local mayor continued to enforce Ubico's vagrancy law throughout 1946. In contrast, in many Kaqchikel communities the effects were immediate and disruptive (Grandin 2004: 38–39). In Sololá, for example, by 1945 police officers, municipal employees, and other officials were regularly being reprimanded for failing to perform their duties according to the standards of the new government; many were threatened with dismissal; some were fired. The Sololá municipal archives from this era illustrate the growing pains of a municipality trying to adapt to a new national government. When the municipal guard Juan José Saenz played religious propaganda over the loudspeaker in the public park on January 29, 1947, he was issued his last warning. So many people were fired or resigned from positions such as Saenz's that the posts became veritable revolving doors. In an indication of local employees' expectations of life after the dictatorship, many of the complaints were attributed to a lack of discipline. On August 2, 1950, for example, Carlota Romero was reprimanded for socializing with employees instead of doing her own work. She too received a thinly veiled threat of dismissal if she did not attend to her own tasks, in her own office. By the end of the month, the mayor felt it necessary to issue specific guidelines for workplace conduct. To avoid the problem of people conversing in each others' doorways, he demanded that employees remain in their offices whether or not they had work to do. He also reminded employees that the municipality was apolitical and as such they were not to talk about politics or political candidates in the municipal building. Anyone who disobeyed these guidelines would be fired (Archivo Municipal de Sololá, 1946–50).

Though some municipal officials and employees like those in Comalapa, where they celebrated the "glorious revolution of 1944" as late as 1950, clearly welcomed the transition, others resisted the new government's attempt to impose its system and ideology on their lives and work (Archivo Municipal de Comalapa 1949–1950). If the municipal records in Sololá are any indication, many struggled to find their way in Guatemala's nascent democracy. The break in the archival record in 1950 leaves the historian to wonder if employees eventually conformed to the new government as they had with the dictatorship, thereby learning what they could do within the established parameters and whom they needed to appease to achieve their goals.

Because the state was not an entity that could be trusted, democracy did not necessarily hold the potential of an improved political system. Indeed, because Guatemala's democracy was born in and begat violence, Kaqchikels' lived experience encouraged them to support strict, strong-armed, consistent, even harsh authoritarians who could maintain stability as opposed to more progressive leaders who in disrupting the status quo may not be able to mitigate the deleterious effects of political freedoms. For many, 1954 simply marked the end of another government—an event that did not necessarily merit particular attention in their historical trajectory.

The 1944 Patzicía Massacre

Ixtoya, a seventy-five-year-old Kaqchikel Patziciana, recalled awakening to the start of the massacre in 1944.

> The people woke up at three or four in the morning because of the *oyowal* [conflict or trouble] in the plaza. All the men took their machetes because the ladinos wanted to finish us off. Ladinos felt that they deserved everything, even the poor man's crops, my dad said. My dad had been in the military. . . . They wanted to finish us off. Then Zaragozanos came, fired on us, and killed our people indiscriminately. Many poor people were born to the Word of God and the earth was filled up with them. The people all left their houses and then we experienced a terrible famine. I was only seven. I could barely lift myself up and I would get tired. My grandmother told me we must move on and look for weeds in Chwako'ok. We will go there on foot with our basket. . . . The *milpa* [corn, bean, and squash plot] was still small. That is how we suffered from famine. You might be lucky to throw a few seeds, or you might find some money, but you owned nothing and you had no corn. (Ixkawoq, Sept. 2001)

On October 22, 1944, just two days after General Federico Ponce Vaides, Ubico's handpicked successor, abdicated the liberal dictatorship under pressure from a movement comprised of students, military reformers, teachers, professionals, urban workers, and an emerging middle class, fighting broke out between Kaqchikels and ladinos in the town of Patzicía; both sides suffered casualties (de León Aragón 1995; Handy 1994: 23; Forster 2001: 33–34). Against the tide of the largely urban ladino popular sentiment of freedom and democracy, these Kaqchikels wanted to ensure they received the benefits the liberal party had promised them, particularly their land rights. Based on their experience with previous governments, they had no reason to trust a new group of ladino leaders. Led by Trindidad Esquit Morales, a lieutenant in the army, about twenty-five Kaqchikels armed with machetes, stones, and axes gathered to support Ponce and to protest ladino domination of local resources.

In response to the chaos, a call went out to the nearby ladino town of Zaragoza. Shortly thereafter twenty-two ladinos armed with guns arrived in Patzicía to put down the rebellion. Responding to a machete fight with firepower gave ladinos a tremendous, and ultimately bloody, advantage. More ladinos from Zaragoza and other towns soon followed. Instead of simply capturing the rebels, they sought to round up and kill each Kaqchikel man. As the carnage multiplied, many Kaqchikels fled to the surrounding hills, canyons, and towns. Those who remained hid their male kin. When the civic guard from Antigua and the national army from the capital finally restored order a few days later, between twelve and fourteen ladinos and between sixty and nine hundred Kaqchikels had been killed.[5] Like in the October 22 massacre, Kaqchikels were victimized disproportionately in the subsequent judicial proceedings: thirty-three were arrested, about a dozen of whom were put to death; the others served out lengthy prison sentences. In contrast, no ladinos were ever tried (Esquit 2002: 356n.24; Forster 2001: 93–94). Newspaper coverage reflected these injustices (*El Imparcial* 1944b, 1944c; *Nuestro Diario* 1944a). When the media sanitized ladino violence and depicted Kaqchikels as incompetent, undeserving, even dangerous citizens, they perpetuated images of the Patzicía massacre that resonated with ladino constructions and perceptions of social relations, organization, and order and disorder (Roseberry 1989: 45). The technological advantage in weaponry, the high number of Kaqchikel as opposed to ladino deaths, the anonymity of Kaqchikel victims versus the publicity of ladino victims, and the lopsided legal process were both products and proof of political, economic, social, and judicial structures that privileged ladinos. Because it demonstrates the intensity of racial animosity in Guatemala, the Patzicía massacre remains paramount in both Kaqchikel historical narratives and the nation's collective memory.

Much like other Mayas who lived near the capital, Kaqchikels who began the protest ardently supported the liberal dictatorship of Ubico and his successor, Ponce. In some areas, ladinos and Mayas were united in their support for the liberals. Just a few days before Ubico resigned on July 1, 1944, a group of Kaqchikels and ladinos from San Martín Jilotepeque pledged their support for him against "antipatriotic and despicable elements who try to overthrow public order" (Archivo General de Centro América 1944). In truth, many Kaqchikels from Patzicía feared Arévalo because they believed him to be a "candidate of the ladinos" who would not support or protect Maya interests.

Yet throughout Guatemala, Mayas were divided on their perceptions of the new government. While others sought to undermine it, many welcomed the changes and subsequent land reform, especially in the department of Chimaltenango where Patzicía was located (Adams 1992: 18–19; Forster 2001: 94–94; Grandin 2000: ch. 8; Handy 1994; Carey Jr. 2001: 92–102, 225–233). One group from Tecpán encouraged Mayas to give thanks to the revolutionary junta because it "was turning the country toward constitutionality and maintaining among the people a breath of hope against tyranny" (*Nuestro Diario* 1944b: 7, 15). Similarly, even in Patzicía, where an "indigenous vanguard" invited and helped to create the conditions for change, Mayas were never a monolithic block opposed to democracy. By building their own school and developing a curriculum that celebrated instead of denigrated Mayas in the 1920s and 1930s, Kaqchikel leaders modeled a new national potential for Guatemala (Rodas and Esquit 1997; Carey Jr. 2001: 165–167). The efficacy of such efforts sparked ladino ire. Born and raised in Patzicía, Ixtz'unun recalled:

> My dad told me a lot of history from Patzicía. In 1944, the troubles in Patzicía erupted over land with the village of Zaragoza. They killed my great grandfather. My grandfather was taken to jail and died three years later due to inflammation. My dad never really knew him. Many people died because of the *oyowal. It was the indigenous race against the ladino race. . . .* when Ubico left and Arévalo arrived. Another reason was the *alcaldes* [mayors] were always indigenous and the ladinos wanted a ladino alcalde to control the town. Moreover, our people founded a school just for themselves. . . . [Ladinos] did not want our people to have studies. They do not want us to develop. (August 29, 1998, Comalapa, emphasis added)

Many Kaqchikels describe the Patzicía *oyowal* as a race war that escalated to genocide. "They wanted to finish us off. Many died. They thrust in and pushed the women down when they could not find the men. The ladinos had guns. We only killed one of them. And they weren't just here for four days; it lasted a while. They tried to finish us off," noted Ixq'axel, who was only four years old at the time (June 23, 2004, Patzicía (Ixkawoq)). Ixb'oq,' a woman from Tecpán, added, "[During the] Patzicía *oyowal*, they killed our people in their homes because they did not want Kaqchikel spoken" (May 31, 1998, Tecpán). By undermining the political stability Mayas appreciated under Ubico's authoritarian but predictable rule, the transition to democracy created the conditions for ladinos to lash out.

Even though the numbers in the municipal death registry a few days after the massacre are almost certainly low, the sixty-one (mostly Kaqchikel) deaths from gunshots reveal the media's estimates to be far below what the community suffered. And of course, these immediate mortalities only tell part of the story. Patzicía continued to display unusually high mortality rates in the months following the massacre (Archivo Municipal de Patzicía 1944a). For the survivors, dealing with the emotional and psychological effects of the massacre took a heavy toll on their physical health. As Manuel Juárez Monasterio explained to the court on December 8, 1944: "My grandmother Juana Monasterio is suffering from mental illness as a result of her advanced age and the impression that the miserable events . . . in Patzicía on 22 October of this year left on her spirit. She has some good days, but during the rest she says incoherent things" (Archivo Municipal de Patzicía 1944b).

The Massacre as an Historical Watershed

Since fear of ladino or state violence or both is a recurrent theme in Kaqchikel history (Esquit 2002: 167–168; Carey Jr. 2001: 117–118), the Patzicía massacre can be read as an historical juncture that informs Kaqchikel perceptions of ethnic and state relations both before and after 1944. It was a harrowing harbinger to the ethnic violence and genocide that erupted during Guatemala's civil war. The stories of Patzicianas who fled to other towns or tried to hide their association with Patzicía as a result of the massacre both informed and reflected such Maya survival strategies as emigration and assimilation during the civil war. In an indication of Kaqchikels' low expectations of ladinos, some Kaqchikels maintained that the events in 1944 are evidence that sixty years later ethnic relations have improved.[6] The sixty-one-year-old Ixchoy asserted: "We have forgotten about Zaragoza and Patzicía. But people who really felt it will never forget. Those who lived it and saw it will not forget. . . . For them, their friends and family died. I did not see it so I do not feel badly [about it]. Now life is joyful. But ladinos have always treated us poorly. They hit us in the road. They say all kinds of things to us. Now things have improved, but previously they hit us a lot" (June 30, 2001, Patzicía). Even though Ixchoy claims she has forgotten the Patzicía massacre, it triggers memories of ladino disparagement and abuse.

Kaqchikel descriptions of the Patzicía massacre and the civil war, which intensified in the Kaqchikel highlands in the late 1970s and early 1980s, have an eerie resonance; comments like "They tried to finish us off" are common in narratives of both. Such connections between those two violent episodes intimate why 1954 is not paramount in Kaqchikel narratives of the past. According to Kaqchikel historical reconstructions, Guatemala's modern crisis did not originate with the U.S. intervention, but rather can be traced to the country's deep historical roots of ethnic animosity, exploitation, and violence.

And of course for some Guatemalans, the CIA facilitated what they wanted. Though the brainchild of the CIA, the 1954 coup enjoyed some support in Guatemala. While Movimiento de Liberación Nacional (MLN) activists worked closely with the CIA, Arbenz's opponents also included ladino professionals, creole elites, Catholic bishops, and middle-class Mayas among others (Grandin 2004: 86–87, 2000: 211–219). For these Guatemalans, the coup was not a cataclysmic event. Nor was it for Kaqchikels whose memories of the 1944 massacre were still raw in 1954.

As with any group of disparate people, perceptions of political leaders varied among Kaqchikels, yet many shared a sense that the state often did not have the capacity or willingness to protect them. "There was a lot of killing when he [Arévalo] came into office. I was thirteen years old when they slaughtered the people in Patzicía. . . . But I think Ubico did it, not Arévalo. He was a good man. Arévalo made peace. You did not hear about any more violence when he came in," remembered Ixya', a seventy-three-year-old woman from Comalapa (April 11, 1998, Comalapa). Ixsinkal, an eighty-year-old woman from Patzún, recalled: "It started with one dead, until the poor people had to hide. Many went to the forest to hide. People in Patzún hid others here [in our community]. Perhaps the president did it. I forget how it started, but many died. . . . They did *la violencia* in Patzicía. . . . Yes, Patzicía was finished off" (July 18, 2003, Patzún [Ixkawoq]). By implicating national leaders, these last two accounts illustrate a distrust of the state. Like other Kaqchikel raconteurs, these Kaqchikel women did not harbor a sense of false consciousness but rather recognized the tensions between their communities and the state.[7] Neither woman could recollect precisely how the massacre began, but both were quick to assume a president played some role in it. The state's history of exploitation and abuse prior to 1944 and the military's role in targeting Maya communities during the civil war convinced many that the state must have been part of the problem because its "essence was alien and dangerous" (Levenson-Estrada 1994: 67).

Because Kaqchikel narrators look back on the past through the filter of the civil war, the capricious and wanton state violence in the 1970s and 1980s made the Ubico dictatorship look good in comparison.[8] Even though most Kaqchikel informants did not associate the democratic government with the Patzicía massacre, by not preventing or responding swiftly and decisively to it, the revolutionary regime violated the social contract Ubico had established with Kaqchikels and Mayas more broadly. Though Kaqchikel elders maintained a critical view of Ubico, most hailed his blind and harsh approach to justice. According to elders, criminals and especially murderers were punished (the latter with capital punishment) regardless of their ethnicity (Carey Jr. 2001: 206–208). The Arévalo administration's failure to bring ladino perpetrators of the massacre to justice undermined its reputation in the eyes of many Kaqchikels. Not unique to the Arévalo administration, such violations of the social contract so discouraged Kaqchikels that they came to expect little of the state and its forms (except perhaps the judicial system); instead they often put their hopes in individuals who they believed would overturn or at least attenuate unjust structures.

Violence and discrimination bolstered a system that privileged ladinos. Ixki'ch, a Kaqchikel artist, noted, "Ladinos are bad and they made bad laws. If you did something they did not like, they would kill you" (June 27, 2001, Comalapa). Kaqchikels recognize that Guatemala's injustice is based on racist structures—legal, political, economic, and social—and the state's and ladinos' willingness to use physical force to uphold them. Illustrating the normalization of ladino abuse, Ixtoya, a seventy-five-year-old Kaqchikel widow, recalled: "[One time] we met ladinos on the way to Parramos. We were eight to twelve girls walking and none of us was thrown down, not even one. That was happiness in those days" (September 2001, Patzicía [Ixkawoq]). Because it discriminated against Mayas and upheld structures that exploited them, the state lost credibility in the eyes of many Mayas and thereby undermined its hegemony. "In the past here the government did not value indigenous people. They said we were at fault because indigenous people are backwards. But that is not true," added Ixroquel (June 29, 2001, Comalapa). Though they could not radically change the Guatemalan state, Kaqchikel perceptions of it as morally bankrupt encouraged their resistance to it.

Fledgling Democracies and Distinct Hegemonies

This lack of confidence in the political system and government continues to affect national life today. One poll revealed that Guatemalans have less trust in democracy than the citizens of any other Latin American nation. Participation in national elections between 1984 and 1999 dropped from 78 percent to 40 percent and dipped as low as 12 percent (Hernández Pico 1999: 16; Azpuru 1999: 6–7, 1994; Torres-Rivas 1999: 51). The national electoral process indicates that a large segment of the population feels alienated from the state. "The government does not work well. For example, now we have eleven languages in our constitution but we only use one [Spanish]. We fail to comply with what we have," argued Oxi' Q'anil, a Kaqchikel ethnohistorian (June 26, 1999, Comalapa). The 2004 protests in Guatemala over the Central American Free Trade Agreement (CAFTA) point to other sources of disillusionment. When government officials and business elites negotiated CAFTA's terms behind closed doors and then announced them at a hotel, a space to which poor Mayas and ladinos only had access as low-wage laborers, it was clear that working-class Guatemalans remained on the margins of democracy. Ka'i' Imox, an eighty-three-year-old campesino, lamented: "The government does not help the poor Indians. They let us die in the mud. We contribute but we do not benefit. The government gives its own people and the wealthy jobs through the military, public positions, hospitals, et cetera and we just perform our forced labor or pay taxes" (June 26, 1999, Comalapa). Though Ka'i' Imox's reflections are informed by a lived experience that extends back to the early twentieth century, Maya exclusion from Guatemala's democracy can be traced to its birth in 1944.

To discredit Patziciana insurgents in 1944, newspaper accounts stated that in addition to land, the liberal party leader Bernardo Méndez promised Kaqchikel loyalists that "the women ladinas would be for them" (*Nuestro Diario* 1944a; *Impacto* 1977). Reports such as these effectively portrayed women as spoils and Mayas as savages. Though the apex of such gratuitous depictions of violence was an artist's sketch of a Kaqchikel man beheading a nine-year-old ladino boy (a fictitious event) published in *El Imparcial* (1944a, 1944d), in general the press presented Kaqchikels as ignorant, lacking in political judgment, and tending toward violence and plunder. In this way, the media posited that Kaqchikels (and by extension all Mayas) were not ready for broad participatory politics, nor did they merit political representation.

Ironically, the lessons Kaqchikels gleaned from the Patzicía massacre were similar to those articulated by ladino journalists and leaders. Looking back, many Kaqchikels believed that Guatemala—though not Mayas in particular, as journalists argued—was not yet ready for democracy, which therefore was not particularly alluring to them. B'eleje' K'at explained: "Democracy is disorder. You need some time to develop it" (November 5, 1997, Comalapa).[9] For some, freedom engendered chaos. "When Arévalo became president, he gave freedom. There was no pressure so that is when laziness began. If you did not want to work, then you did not. But with Ubico, all had to work or they were punished. [With Arévalo] people became increasingly lazy and then came the time of violence," observed one group of men (B'eleje' Tz'i', Junlajuj B'atz', and Junlajuj Toj, May 20, 1998, Xetonox, Comalapa). Even those within the local political establishment who welcomed democracy and lauded Arévalo felt the populace was ill-prepared for this shift. "Arévalo was the best president. He gave us rights, but then it fell apart. Too many thieves took advantage of it all," lamented Waqi' Iq', a former mayor of Comalapa (December 12, 1997). If so many Kaqchikels questioned the wisdom of imposing democracy in Guatemala, then it makes sense that its demise does not form a cornerstone of their historical narratives; rather than a tragic missed opportunity, it was simply one failed state in a long history of many.

Accounts that describe Ubico's thirteen-year rule as a halcyon past are evidence of a preference for authoritarianism, which developed not because Kaqchikels were duplicitous but rather because they knew where they stood with certain dictators. These impressions are both informed by and inform Kaqchikel notions that Guatemala is either unsuitable for democracy or should only subscribe to a dictatorial version of it. Even in Guatemala's current manifestation of democracy, caudillolike figures continue to emerge. Take for example this statement by President Alvaro Arzú (1996–2000): "To the delinquents, white-collar criminals, kidnappers, drug traffickers, rapists, agitators, and youth gangs, to all these pariahs of society, I want to say that war is declared" (*Cerigua Weekly Reports* 1997). Though the targets may have changed, his tough talk resonates with Ubico's. The reasons for Ubico's popularity in Guatemalans' historical consciousnesses are complex, but certainly his emphasis on maintaining stability and security boosted his reputation. And his visits to rural communities allowed him to connect with many Mayas. In contrast, though democracy offers participation through voting, many Kaqchikels view the vote not as power but rather as exclusion because, once elected, leaders pursue their own agendas to the detriment of Mayas. If the vote does not hold people accountable, and mostly ladinos are gaining power through it, who will advocate for Maya interests? For many Kaqchikels, if there is no system in place that guarantees their rights and representation proportional to their numbers, then it is better to have a transparent strong-armed leader who can maintain peace and respond to them on an ad hoc basis.

To avoid being confined by a paradigm that presumes democracy is the goal, as scholars we should inquire about what type of political system and structures Mayas envision for their nation. As one example, in her study of the 2007 Guatemalan elections, Rebecca Aubrey found that many Guatemalans believed that political parties were not necessary for democracy (2008). Even though the Guatemalan state often was weak institutionally, the nation as an "imagined community" was strong. But it was not just elites imagining the nation, as Benedict Anderson implies (1991); poor, rural Mayas also had well-developed conceptions of their country and their place in it (Carey Jr. 2006: 156–158; 2004).

Understanding their place in the nation was predicated partly on a keen awareness of the forces and actors that constrained their lives. Kaqchikels made a clear distinction between local ladinos who were immediate oppressors and the state. Anthropologist Kay Warren argues that this distinction developed during the Ubico regime: "Ubico's economic and educational reforms . . . are pointed to as the first evidence of a split in social ideology between the government and the local ladino landholders who had earlier been perceived as politically homogeneous in their desire to control Indians as a subordinate agricultural labor force" (1989: 145). For Kaqchikels, the state is not the same as local ladinos, nor is it the same as government officials, nor is it the same as a dictator or president, nor is it the same as people's recourses. As scholars, we need to unravel distinctions such as these. Identifying local oppressors with the state obscures the way people look for levers with which to contest local relations and work the system to its minimum disadvantage (Hobsbawm 1973: 13).

Gender and the Revolution

As Aj Kanil K'amal B'e, a Maya journalist, wrote in 1995, "The [1944] revolution did not confront the liberation of the indigenous people, as a specific group. The discriminatory prejudices against the Mayas continue in force" (1995). The same could be said for women. Because of their ethnicity and gender, Maya women were largely ignored by the revolutionary government and thus gained little in the shift from Ubico to Arévalo. Though the political effects of the democratic government in local Maya communities varied— some enjoyed increased Maya control of local political offices, while in others Maya political representation remained negligent largely because local ladinos refused to recognize the 1945 constitution—Maya women's political experience was almost universal. Since congress granted suffrage to illiterate men (in the form of an oral vote) but only literate women in 1945, the majority of Maya women remained disenfranchised (Handy 1994: 24, 43–44, 52, 131; 1988: 703, 706; 1990: 147, 178–179; 1984: 167–171; Reina 1972: 32; Adams 1970: 187–189; Silvert and King 1972: 44–47; Ebel 1972: 189–190; Forster 2001: 2). In this way, the revolutionary government reinforced patriarchal structures in Maya communities. *Cofradías, alcaldías* (mayors' offices), and most other traditional and official positions remained the exclusive domain of men. In short, democracy failed to challenge gendered structures or relations of power in Maya communities. If representation in Guatemala's burgeoning democracy was only for males or literate females, then illiterate Maya women not only were denied participation, they were unrepresentable. In effect, the democratic governments declared that illiterate (predominantly Maya) women were not appropriate protagonists (Taylor 1997: 88–89). Since most Maya women did not gain any rights that they subsequently could have lost in 1954, the coup had little immediate effect on their lived experience. Kaqchikel women expanded their rights and mobility by their own devices, not through any larger political movement.

Because of their long history of disenfranchisement, most Kaqchikel female interlocutors claim ignorance of politics. The consistency of women's exclusion from local political power is striking. Even while Kaqchikel women such as Rosalina Tuyúc and Aura Marina Otzoy emerged as national leaders in congress in the 1990s, no female mayors ever have been elected in the Kaqchikel towns of Comalapa, Tecpán, Poaquil, or Patzicía, to cite a few (though in 2004 Irma Goméz declared her candidacy in Patzicía's municipal elections). Even during major transitions on the national scene, local political systems changed little for women. That gendered constructions of authority and public importance remained largely entrenched in Maya communities reveals one of the ways in which sociopolitical foundations were consistent before, during, and after the reigns of Arévalo and Arbenz. This reality, coupled with Kaqchikel women's assertion that the 1954 coup did not catalyze the civil war, explains why Kaqchikel female raconteurs largely ignored the events of 1954 in their historical narratives.

In contrast, in both Kaqchikel women's and men's oral histories, the Patzicía massacre has come to symbolize the apogee of ethnic tensions, which extend both backward and forward from 1944. It serves as a nexus for past, present, and future accounts of relations between ladinos and Kaqchikels. Ixxovin, a seventy-six-year-old woman from Patzicía, noted, "Ladinos have not liked us for a long time now. They did the *oyowal* here. The *oyowal* proves it. That is why they did the *oyowal,* because they do not like us. Ladinos abuse *indios*" (August 23, 2003, Patzicía [Ixkawoq]). Her account of ethnic relations moves from the past to the present through the Patzicía *oyowal.* This historical juncture triggers Kaqchikel narratives of ladinos who outwardly displayed their disrespect for Mayas by hitting them, spitting at them, and calling them racially charged derogatory names like *indio* or *ixto.* "There were problems because ladinos did not like to look at us. They felt they were more worthy than us because they had different clothes and spoke Spanish," explained the fifty-three year-old Ixkatu (June 28, 2001, Comalapa [Ixch'onïk]). The Patzicía massacre can be seen as an explosive expression of the physical aggression ladinos felt privileged to inflict upon Kaqchikels daily. Tragically, many ladinos reasserted physical intimidation as a viable threat in the post-1954 state.

As Patzicía Goes, So Goes the Nation

The reverberations of the Patzicía massacre loomed large in the historical consciousness of Guatemala. Newspapers warned of other imminent Maya uprisings that, though they seldom materialized and never on the scale of Patzicía's, struck fear in many ladinos (Carey Jr. 2006). As a bellwether of unrest, the 1944 massacre was an excuse to curtail Maya efforts to organize elsewhere. Just a few years later, the ladino mayor of Tecpán confronted a group of Kaqchikel Catholic Action (an orthodox movement) advocates because "the town believed [they] were organizing an uprising of indigenous people and that they were going to take the *cabecera municipal* [municipal capital] like the indigenous people of Patzicía had done a few kilometers from Tecpán" (Cabarrús Pellecer 1998: 91). Perhaps the alcalde's concern was warranted. During the 1950s and 1960s, Catholic Action spurred confrontations, some of which turned violent, in a number of Maya communities (*Prensa Libre* 1967; Ix'echa,' September 9, 1998, Santa Cruz Balanya; Ixtz'i,' September 12, 1998, Comalapa; Esquit 2002: 156n110; Cabarrús Pellecer 1998: 91–103; Warren 1989: 97–113; Carmack 1995: 239–241; Carlsen 1997: 124–125). Beginning in the 1970s, civil strife became a deadly endemic. In a prescient observation on the thirty-third anniversary of the massacre and the eve of Guatemala's genocidal campaigns of the early 1980s, one writer warned, "If things in Guatemala continue as they are, we are not far from having another 'Patzicía' on a national level. We must avoid that" (*Impacto* 1977).[10] That the article was reprinted in 1986 shortly after Marco Vinicio Cerezo

Arévalo (1986–91) became the first civilian to become president since 1970 in a procedurally correct election largely free of fraud, was evidence that even as Guatemala was taking this renewed step toward democracy, the political environment remained fragile and violent.

Patzicía is a microcosm of the effects of the nation's failure to confront its past. Just as ladinos who killed Kaqchikels in Patzicía were never tried for murder, most perpetrators of human rights abuses during the civil war are still living alongside their victims and their families in Guatemala today.[11] Ixtz'unun noted: "One family from Zaragoza that did a lot of killing now lives in Patzicía, and I do not like to see them because their descendants did the killing. Some of those who murdered are still around, they do not die. . . . that is why they killed E——-because they did not want *qawináq* to have studies. They do not want us to develop. So they killed him. . . . There are still conflicts and discrimination. They call you María or *noya,* but now you correct them and tell them you have a name and not to call you that" (August 29, 1998, Comalapa). When murderers' and victims' families share neighborhoods, the process of building a harmonious postconflict society must include official recognition of, if not restitution for, the crimes. To date, neither has happened in Patzicía or Guatemala.

Conclusion

My goal has been not to argue for the primacy of the Patzicía massacre in Kaqchikel historical consciousness, but rather to use the massacre as a point of comparison to highlight the obscurity of the 1954 coup in Kaqchikel reconstructions of the past. For Mayas, as for most people, local experiences and threats are as important as national (and international) ones. In turn, the Patzicía massacre did not necessarily resonate with other Maya communities. Indeed, even though it is prevalent in their oral histories, Comalapenses did not portray it in their historical murals. Informed by historical narratives that extend back multiple generations, most Kaqchikels perceive the state as wanton, unjust, dangerous, and capricious. As a result, changes in its political systems are less important to them than who is at the helm. Even Kaqchikel men attracted to the idea of democracy have had little faith that it could be implemented safely and successfully in Guatemala. And for illiterate Maya women, democracy was simply another system by which men on both the national and local levels maintained control over public positions of power. Based on such Kaqchikel historical sources as oral histories, murals, and textiles, the historical pattern of violent manifestations of ladino racism, women's disenfranchisement, and the 1976 earthquake—whose geological rumblings often further disrupted political and social tensions, for example—go further in explaining Guatemala's recent past, at least for Kaqchikels, than the 1954 coup.

In taking a suggestive rather than a prescriptive stance, I hope to point out the need for further research that incorporates, even privileges, Maya perspectives. Doing so might help us rethink the very premise of this book. Not that it should not be written—certainly the research is vital to understanding the effects of the cold war in Guatemala and throughout Latin America, U.S. policy in the region (and world), state-community political relations, and the shifting fields of power between subaltern and hegemon, among other topics. But we should seek to produce scholarship that Mayas and other Guatemalans would recognize as both authoritative and relevant. To be authoritative, we need to understand how they would frame the history of the second half of the twentieth century. But we also need to address epistemological questions. For instance, if most Mayas recognize knowledge and information that is passed on through oral tradition as the most trustworthy and valid, how will they perceive findings based largely on newly declassified U.S. government documents? How can Maya ways of knowing and the consultation of Maya elders be incorporated into the analysis of these documents? For our work to be relevant, we need to know what Mayas would like to do with the information, which of course requires that it be disseminated among them in formats they can digest. In addition to being consulted as experts, Mayas should also be an explicit part of the intended audience.

Even when thinking about the uses to which a U.S. audience might put these findings, we should be cognizant of Maya perspectives. For instance, could this scholarship be used to present a case for or against CAFTA? (For example, reflecting on the United Fruit Company's influence in 1954 could shed light on the roles multinational corporations may play with CAFTA.) Might it help to expose the pitfalls of contemporary U.S. foreign policy (not just in Latin America)? Or would Mayas encourage us to be less preoccupied with the U.S. role, and instead to develop a broader understanding of the multiple forces at play?

Paradoxically, perhaps as U.S. scholars critical of our own government, we overstate the influence of our nation. Is much of our scholarship guilty of the solipsistic assumption that U.S. involvement in 1954 was paramount?[12] Are we overestimating the importance of the coup in the eyes of Guatemalans in 1954 and today? Certainly Kaqchikel interlocutors and June Nash's chapter in this book suggest as much. To gain an appreciation of the interplay between local, national, and international forces that largely determined Guatemala's modern history, we must achieve some balance between the multiplicity of perspectives in oral as well as archival accounts. The panoply of Maya voices, including Maya refugees and immigrants, about a million of whom currently reside in the United States, is a crucial source not only for understanding how the drastic change in the political climate after 1954 affected popular memory and indigeneity in Guatemala, but also how it influenced the social, political, cultural, and economic contexts that shape discourses of power.

The same Kaqchikel historical narratives that compel us to reconsider the significance of the 1954 coup also encourage historical revision of the Ten Years of Spring (1944–54). Just months before the Patzicía massacre, many of its victims had been marching through the capital armed with machetes to support the dictatorship. The Patzicía massacre can be read as a response to this and other public manifestations of indigenous influence such as the mounted, machete-brandishing Mayas who General Ponce set up on the outskirts of the capital to break up protests against the dictatorship in 1944 (Woodward 1985: 231). For ladinos from Zaragoza and Patzicía, the massacre was about putting *indios* back in their place. Though Arévalo never articulated such a sentiment, neither did he officially condemn the massacre. Compared to Ubico, Arévalo was far removed from a political coalition capable of understanding rural indigenous politics. In contrast to the dominant trend in Guatemalan historiography that portrays the Ten Years of Spring as a welcome reprieve from a series of dictators, Arévalo's democratic government often suffers a poorer reputation than its dictatorial predecessors in Kaqchikel historical perspectives. The Patzicía massacre indicates that the proverbial springtime in Guatemalan politics did not merely exclude Mayas momentarily; they were pushed out and back in their place. If Maya historical perspectives and national imaginings are to be taken seriously, then this interpretation suggests that historians should go at least as far back as 1944 in looking for the seeds of Guatemala's modern maelstrom.

Acknowledgments

I wish to thank the conference participants and audience for their critical comments on my original paper. This final version has benefited greatly from a careful reading by Edward Fischer, Michael Stone, David Stoll, and one anonymous reviewer for University of Illinois Press. I am indebted to the municipal officials at the Archivo Municipal de Sololá, Archivo Municipal de Patzicía, and Archivo Municipal de San Juan Comalapa for their efforts and insights. I am especially grateful to my oral history research assistants, Ixch'onïk and Ixkawoq, and to the Kaqchikel raconteurs who shared their time and historical knowledge and analysis. The University of Southern Maine and the American Historical Association generously provided funding for this research.

Notes

Parts of this chapter were published in Carey Jr. 2006, ch. 4.

1. As Arturo Taracena Arriola points out, during the colonial period Creoles and ladinos allied with each other because they feared Mayas (1997).

2. Many Kaqchikel distinguished their perceptions of Ubico and Barrios from their assessment of the state itself. For an analysis of the complex and at times contradictory Kaqchikel historical perspectives of national leaders like Ubico and Barrios, see Carey Jr. (2001, ch. 6 and 7).

3. Due to Guatemala's continued political volatility and recurrent human rights abuses, I have preserved the anonymity of my sources for their safety. For the most part, I have used names that derive from the Maya calendar. Female informants can be recognized by the "Ix" prefix to their one-word names. In contrast, male names have two words. A name in parentheses after the informant's citation indicates that one of my Kaqchikel research assistants (Ixch'onïk or Ixkawoq) conducted the interview; I performed all other interviews. All oral history interviews were performed in Kaqchikel in the communities where informants lived, and most often in their homes.

4. Though a bit confused as to the details of the roles of the Dulles brothers, Lajuj Kame's point that the close ties between the United Fruit Company and the U.S. government spelled doom for Guatemala's democracy is well taken. Allen Dulles was the director of the CIA from 1953 to 1961. His brother John Foster Dulles, whose law firm represented the United Fruit Company, was the secretary of state under President Dwight D. Eisenhower from 1953 to 1959. It is also interesting to note, that according to Lajuj Kame, most Kaqchikel and the United States shared the desire for a caudillo; they just differed on what qualities that person should have.

5. The estimates of Maya deaths vary greatly, but two independent studies indicate that somewhere between four hundred and nine hundred Kaqchikel were killed during the three-day massacre. See Rodas and Esquit (1997: 195) and Adams (1992: 16–18, 23).

6. Adams draws the same conclusion from his interlocutors (1992: 20–22).

7. For a cogent critique of the notion that hegemony is grounded partly in false consciousness see Scott (1985: 317–350).

8. At the same time, the intensity of the civil war did not erase critiques of the Ubico, Arévalo, or Arbenz regimes. Kaqchikel judgments of leaders were seldom absolute. Although she associates Ubico with the massacre, Ixya,' for example, believed Arévalo, if not the state under his rule, to be fair and efficacious.

9. Historian Steve Stern heard similar misgivings about President Salvador Allende's attempt to introduce a socialist government in Chile in 1970: the "pueblo . . . was not prepared for it" (2004: 83).

10. The worst of the violence and what the United Nations defined as genocide occurred under the regimes of General Fernando Romeo Lucas García (1978–82) and General José Efraín Ríos Montt (1982–83) from September 1981 to October 1982, when the military massacred residents of hundreds of Maya communities, many of which were subsequently wiped off the map. See CEH (Comisión para el Esclaracimiento Histórico) 1999; ODHAG (Oficina de Derechos Humanos del Arzobispado de Guatemala) 1999; Falla 1992.

11. Of course, one crucial aspect sets Patzicía apart from the civil war: in 1944 popular groups perpetrated the violence, whereas during the civil war the military engineered attacks on the population.

12. See for example, Immerman (1982); Schlesinger and Kinzer (1983); Cullather (1999).

Works Cited

Adams, Richard N.
  1970 Crucifixion by Power: Essays on Guatemalan National Social Structure, 1944–1966. Austin and London: University of Texas Press.
  1992 Las masacres de Patzicía de 1944. Revista Winak Boletín Intercultural (Guatemala: Universidad Mariano Gálvez) 7(1–4) (June): 3–40.
Aj Kanil K'amal B'e
  1995 ¿Que significó para el pueblo Maya la revolución de 1944? Rutzijol: por la autogestión del Pueblo Maya 7(8)7 Kame ka 8 Ajpu (July 30–August 13).
Anderson, Benedict
  1991 Imagined Communities: Reflections on the Origin and Spread of Nationalism. London: Verso.
Archivo General de Centro América
  1944 Jefatura Política, Chimaltenango, leg. 88A. Carta a comandante General don Jorge Ubico, presidente de la República de la Municipalidad de San Martín Jilotepeque, 26 de junio 1944.
Archivo Municipal de Patzicía (AMP)
  1944a Libro de Fallecimientos 16.
  1944b Packet 126. Manuel Juárez Monasterio petition to Jefe Político, December 8.
Archivo Municipal de San Juan Comalapa
  1949–50 Municipalidad de San Juan Comalapa Libro para actas de sesiones ordinarias y extraordinarias Comenzando el 2 de marzo de 1949 terminando el 12 de dic de 1950. Unpublished MS.

Archivo Municipal de Sololá
1937–50 "'Libro numero 01.'" Acuerdos y sesiones municipales del 1/03/37 al 28/11/50. Book 1. Unpublished MS.

Aubrey, Rebecca
2008 From MAIZ to Police: Guerillas, Security, and Social Democracy in the 2007 Guatemalan Elections. Paper presented at the New England Council of Latin American Studies Annual Fall Meeting, Brown University, Providence, R.I., October 4.

Azpuru, Dinorah
1994 Estudio de la realidad politica de Guatemala. Guatemala: Universidad Rafael Landívar.
1999 The Consulta Popular: A Vote Divided by Geography. Latin American Program Working Papers Series. Washington, D.C.: Woodrow Wilson International Center for Scholars.

Cabarrús Pellecer, Carlos Rafael
1998 En la conquista del ser: un estudio de identidad étnica. Guatemala: CEDIM-FAFO.

Carey, David, Jr.
2001 Our Elders Teach Us: Maya-Kaqchikel Historical Perspectives. Xkib'ij kan qate' qatata'. Tuscaloosa: University of Alabama Press, 2001.
2004 Mayan Perspectives of the 1999 Referendum in Guatemala: Ethnic Equality Rejected? Latin American Perspectives 31(6) (November): 69–95.
2006 Engendering Mayan History: Kaqchikel Women as Agents and Conduits of the Past 1875–1970. New York: Routledge Press.

Carlsen, Robert
1997 The War for the Heart and Soul of a Highland Maya Town. Austin: University of Texas Press.

Carmack, Robert
1995 Rebels of Highland Guatemala: The Quiche-Mayas of Momostenango. Norman: University of Oklahoma Press.

CEH (Comisión para el Esclaracimiento Histórico)
1999 Guatemala: memoria del silencio. Informe para el esclarecimiento histórico. Guatemala: CEH.

Cerigua Weekly Reports
1997 No. 29, July 31.

Cullather, Nick
1999 Secret History: The CIA's Classified Account of its Operations in Guatemala, 1952–1954. Stanford: Stanford University Press.

de León Aragón, Oscar
1995 Caída de un régimen: Jorge Ubico–Federico Ponce, 20 de octubre 1944. Guatemala: Facultad Latinoamerica de Ciencias Sociales.

Ebel, Roland H.

1972   Political Modernization in Three Guatemalan Indian Communities. *In* Community Culture and National Change. Richard N. Adams, ed. Pp. 131–206. New Orleans: Middle American Research Institute, Tulane University, publication 24.

Esquit, Edgar

1996   Relaciones de poder en Patzicía, 1871–1944. Estudios Interetnicos: revista del Instituto de Estudios Interetnicos. 4(5) (October): 55–75.

2002   Otros poderes, nuevos desafíos: relaciones interétnicas en Tecpán y su entorno departamental (1871–1935). Guatemala: Magna Terra Editores.

Falla, Ricardo

1992   Masacres de la selva: Ixcán, Guatemala 1975–1982. Guatemala: AVANCSO.

Forster, Cindy

2001   The Time of Freedom: Campesino Workers in Guatemala's October Revolution. Pittsburgh, Penna.: University of Pittsburgh Press.

Gillin, John

1958   San Luis Jilotepeque. Guatemala: Seminario de Integración Social Guatemalteca.

Grandin, Greg

2000   The Blood of Guatemala: A History of Race and Nation. Durham, N.C.: Duke University Press.

2004   The Last Colonial Massacre: Latin America in the Cold War. Chicago: University of Chicago Press.

Handy, Jim

1984   Gift of the Devil: A History of Guatemala. Boston: South End Press.

1988   National Policy, Agrarian Reform, and the Corporate Community during the Guatemalan Revolution, 1944–54. Comparative Studies in Society and History 30 (October): 698–724.

1990   The Corporate Community, Campesino Organizations, and Agrarian Reform: 1950–1954. *In* Guatemalan Indians and the State: 1540–1988. Carol A. Smith, ed. Pp. 163–182. Austin: University of Texas Press.

1994   Revolution in the Countryside: Rural Conflict and Agrarian Reform in Guatemala, 1944–1954. Chapel Hill: University of North Carolina Press.

Hernández Pico, Juan

1999   Why Was the Referendum Defeated? Envio. July 1999.

Hobsbawm, E. J.

1973   Peasants and Politics. Journal of Peasant Studies 1(1):3–22.

Immerman, Richard H.

1982   The CIA in Guatemala. Austin: University of Texas Press.

Impacto

1977   La rebellion de los indios. October 23:1.

El Imparcial
1944a   Sketch, October 24.
1944b   Inexorable cae la vindicta contra asesinos de Patzicía. November 18:1,3.
1944c   Recurso de apelación puesto por la defensa de los reos de Patzicia. November 25:1.
1944d   Evocase en todo su terror el asalto indígena contra la población de Itzapa. November 30:1,7.

Levenson-Estrada, Deborah
1994   Trade Unionists against Terror: Guatemala City, 1954–1985. Chapel Hill: University of North Carolina Press.

Nuestro Diario
1944a   La tragedia de Patzicía: nuevos datos que agregar a nuestro info anterior. October 30:8,12.
1944b   Hermanos indígenas. November 18:7,15.

ODHAG (Oficina de Derechos Humanos del Arzobispado de Guatemala)
1999   Guatemala: Never Again! The Official Report of the Recovery of Historical Memory Project (REMHI), Human Rights Office, Archdiocese of Guatemala. Maryknoll, N.Y.: Orbis Books.

Prensa Libre
1967   Motín en Comalapa. December 29:11.

Reina, Rubén E.
1972   Chinautla, a Guatemalan Indian Community. *In* Community Culture and National Change. Richard N. Adams, ed. Pp. 55–130. New Orleans: Middle American Research Institute, Tulane University, publication 24.

Rodas, Isabel, and Edgar Esquit
1997   Élite ladina-vanguardia indígena: de tolerancia a la violencia, Patzicía 1944. Guatemala: CAUDAL.

Roseberry, William
1989   Anthropologies and Histories: Essays in Culture, History, and Political Economy. New Brunswick, N.J.: Rutgers University Press.

Sanders, James E.
2004   Contentious Republicans: Popular Politics, Race, and Class in Nineteenth-Century Colombia. Durham, N.C.: Duke University Press.

Schlesinger, Stephen, and Stephen Kinzer
1983   Bitter Fruit. New York: Doubleday and Anchor Books.

Scott, James C.
1985   Weapons of the Weak: Everyday Forms of Peasant Resistance. New Haven, Conn.: Yale University Press.

Silvert, Kalman H., and Arden R. King
1972   Cobán: 1944–53. *In* Community Culture and National Change. Richard N. Adams, ed. New Orleans: Middle American Research Institute, Tulane University, publication 24.

Smith, Carol A.

1990   Origins of the National Question in Guatemala: A Hypothesis. *In* Guatemalan Indians and the State: 1540–1988. Carol A. Smith, ed. Pp. 72–96. Austin: University of Texas Press.

Stern, Steve

2004   Remembering Pinochet's Chile: On the Eve of London. Durham, N.C.: Duke University Press.

Taracena Arriola, Arturo

1997   Invención criolla, sueño ladino, pesadilla indígena: Los Altos de Guatemala, de region a Estado, 1740–1850. Antigua, Guatemala: Centro de Investigaciones Regionales de Mesoamérica.

Taylor, Diane

1997   Disappearing Acts: Spectacles of Gender and Nationalism in Argentina's "Dirty War." Durham, N.C.: Duke University Press.

Torres Rivas, Edelberto

1999   Peace and Democracy: An Unpredictable Future. Latin American Program Working Papers Series. Washington, D.C.: Woodrow Wilson International Center for Scholars.

Warren, Kay B.

1989[1978]   The Symbolism of Subordination: Indian Identity in a Guatemalan Town. Austin: University of Texas Press.

Woodward, Ralph Lee, Jr.

1985   Central America: A Nation Divided. 2nd ed. Oxford: Oxford University Press.

4

The Politics of Land, Identity, and Silencing

A Case Study from El Oriente of Guatemala, 1944–54

CHRISTA LITTLE-SIEBOLD

The indigenous alcalde received word that the U.S.-backed Colonel Carlos Castillo Armas was to set up camp in Quezaltepeque after invading from neighboring Honduras. The alcalde had to act quickly, with dignity, and in a way that showed the sense of responsibility he felt toward his fellow campesinos. Not all municipalities, particularly in Guatemala's Oriente, had succeeded in electing indigenous mayors during the period of democratic spring (1944–54) after the overthrow of dictator Jorge Ubico y Castañeda (1931–44). Yet because he was one of the few indigenous mayors in the region, Castillo Armas might immediately assume he supported Jacobo Arbenz and have him killed. He decided not to go into hiding. Instead, the alcalde sent word for other leaders to leave as he went to face the colonel and his mercenary army. He shook hands firmly with the coup leader, offered him his own bed, and looked the colonel in the eyes when responding to questions about Quezaltepeque's political alliances. That the invaders killed only one person in Quezaltepeque was a point of pride for the alcalde years later, given the wholesale slaughter of leftist and rural activists that would follow in the weeks and months to come. The alcalde's pride was tinged with regret, though, because the man executed was remembered by fellow townspeople as someone whose life and actions did not merit such an end: a silencing act of public terror that took place on the outskirts of their very own town.

This chapter examines the local politics of land, identity, and memory in Quezaltepeque, Chiquimula, during the Diez Años de Primavera (Ten Years of Spring). Quezaltepeque is where Arbenz's administration ended, as it was the site of Colonel Carlos Castillo Armas's *entrada de la liberación* (assault of the liberation) and march to Guatemala City. The short-lived period of democracy brought about dramatic changes in the political landscape after decades of dictatorship and military rule.

I have pieced together what was going on in a small community in the Eastern Highlands during the ten-year period. Working with consultants, particularly those who were active during the Arévalo and Arbenz administrations, I collected stories about the cattle that went to town, and the saint who went to jail, although he never entered a church. I learned about the local *listas negras* (black lists), and about a few *alcaldes indígenas* (indigenous mayors). These stories are about people—many of whom are still alive—who made local history during those extraordinary years between 1944 and 1954. Their actions still inform the ongoing struggles over land and survival that are embedded in a complex set of racialized identities.[1]

The term that weaves many of the story threads together is *campesino,* a term that reemerged during the Ten Years of Spring. In the midst of so many silences concerning this period, the widely used term *campesino* serves as an ambiguous identity term or "fuzzy category" that positively conflates connotations embraced by rural and town dwellers, indigenous and nonindigenous, progressives and conservatives.

The Place and the People

Quezaltepeque is a municipio of the department of Chiquimula, with its town center nestled in a valley at the edge of a highway that connects Guatemala with El Salvador and Honduras. It is the southeastern edge of the Maya Ch'orti' territory, although the Ch'orti' language has long been lost in the municipio itself. The town center with its *trapiche*-processed sugar cane, and its *vegas* (small fertile valleys) washed with rivers shaded with tropical fruit trees, is a dot of warm, humid emerald green flanked by cool, windy pine forests and grassy high peaks.

Quezaltepeque is in the highlands of Guatemala's Oriente, a geographical and sociological region highly identified in the nationalist imagery with the ladino and with "wild west" stereotypes of lawlessness, cattle, and men. Digging into Quezaltepeque's identity landscape, however, challenges the Guatemalan dichotomy between an "Indian West" and a "Ladino East."[2]

In Quezaltepeque, any accounting of indigenous versus nonindigenous identity that merely draws on visible differences of dress, language, and material life (for example, presence or absence of footwear, house style) obscures a more complicated set of relations. In fact, given the lack of distinguishing visible characteristics (and the loss of spoken Ch'orti' Mayan for several generations), people deploy a nuanced set of terms in which racialized identities intersect with social class, urban/rural referents—and the legacy of the alliances built during the Ten Years of Spring.

Here I explore the most salient terms: *indio, natural, ladino,* and *campesino.* At the time of my research, *indio* was a pervasive term. There was the local self ascription of "soy indio/a" ("I'm an Indian") that reflected the speaker's pride in his or her background. The term *indio/a* was more often than not, however, used as an insult or pejorative endearment. *Indio* was also understood as a racialized identity, referring to skin color, eye color, hair type, name (even if a Spanish surname), and lineage—"blood" as far back as anyone can remember or document.

Many people, urban and rural, referred to themselves and others as *naturales.* The term *natural* has origins in the colonial period and can be used interchangeably with *indio.* The Spaniards used it to refer to "someone born in such and such place," as in a *natural* of Sevilla, or a *natural* of Chimaltenango. In historical documents, however, the term came to signify an Indian, those who were "natural" to the New World, unless it explicitly referred to the place of origin of a Spaniard. Several of Quezaltepeque's late colonial community land titles, for example, refer to the Indians as both *indios* and *naturales.*

In contemporary usage, however, *natural* has come to connote more than a person's place of origin.[3] In the Quezaltepeque of the 1990s, the term was used for anyone with ancestors who fit the local definition of *indígena,* those who wore traditional clothing, such as the *padrinos* and *madrinas* discussed later in this chapter. As younger generations drifted away from the characteristic dress of the indígena, they continued to recognize their indigenous roots yet deployed the more neutral equivalent *natural.* This use of *natural* is not unique to Quezaltepeque but is heard around Guatemala. For example, Maud Oakes (1951: 240) reported the use of the term in 1940s Todos Santos.

The term *natural* is also used by and for those Indians who have adopted a more generic ladino lifestyle. In this way *natural* serves people who do not see themselves as fitting the present-day definitions of *indígena,* as their grandparents had, yet who do not identify with ladinos and their class culture. In fact, a term I rarely heard in the 1990s, *sambo,* used to refer to ladino pretenders, people who abuse power, or arrogant people of white complexion. Therefore, the term *natural* allowed people who, although similar to ladinos in their lack of "lo étnico" (that which is ethnic), recognized themselves as *indígena.*

Other local residents are described by themselves and others as ladinos. But in the region there was more than one route to ladino identification. In the 1990s, there was a whole range of ladinos; those of Spanish, other foreign descent, or upper class or other prestigious social status; people with certain physical features thought of as carried "in the blood." Ladinos generally lived in town, but not all town dwellers were viewed as ladinos by themselves or others. People in Quezaltepeque also identified specific hamlets as ladino enclaves, either because of the residents' "blood lines," perceived ladinolike features (such as blue eyes, skin color, height), or intermarriage with people from adjacent communities considered to be ladino. Individual families that had moved to the countryside, with family ties and property in town, self-ascribed as ladinos as well. Finally, there were *naturales* who either simultaneously or alternatively identified as ladinos.

The term *campesino* is the identity most commonly used for rural dwellers. Whether a person self-ascribed as *natural,* indigenous, or *ladino/a,* all were considered campesinos who shared a livelihood as small-scale family farmers. A ladino/a landholder who lived in the countryside but who did not work the land with their own hands, who employed campesinos and who possessed larger-scale acreage, herds, and farming infrastructure such as grain storage, mills, and vehicles, was not considered campesino.

By the 1990s, when I began my fieldwork, the term *campesino/a* had largely replaced the much-resented term *indio/a* as a referent for rural peoples. People in their sixties or older told me that in the past, when they, their parents, or their grandparents came into town, ladinos called them *indio/a.* At the time of my research, the term *indio/a* was reduced to expressing racialized identity.

Campesino emerged as an identity, I believe, after the fall of Ubico.[4] The label was a strategic semantic tool to draw peasants to the political and social programs of presidents Juan José Arévalo Bermejo (1945–51) and Colonel Jacobo Arbenz Guzmán (1951–54). One Indian alcalde who served during the 1945–54 period said that the rural majority began to use the familiar term *campesino* to express their solidarity and shared land issues.

He also recalled how influential ladino political leaders used the term *campesino* in the formation of the *ligas campesinas* (peasant leagues) and local party chapters. This language was deployed in building up the Confederación Nacional Campesina de Guatemala (CNCG) through the Comisión Agraria Departamental (CAD) and the Comisión Agraria Local (CAL) at the municipal level.[5] The former alcalde recalled how people from Chiquimula, neighboring towns, and even Guatemala City addressed them as *campesino.* To him this was a marked change from the usual pejorative language of the dominant ladino townspeople, who called them *indio/as.* Sympathetic town ladino/as also began to use the term *campesino* during the Ten Years of Spring. Quezaltepeque had a small share of progressive activists committed to the ideals of the Arévalo-Arbenz periods. With the Castillo Armas *entrada,* these individuals, ladinos and *naturales* both, left the area and continued their political work elsewhere. Yet, even with the violent political changes, the more respectful and positive term *campesino* stuck. I assume that with time, the more fashionable and respectful *campesino/a* replaced the loaded term *indio/a;* at the time of my research, individuals who used *indio/a* were seen as old-fashioned and stuck in their ways.

The term may have survived the political changes because of its quality as a "fuzzy classification," as Judith Maxwell (1982: 17) describes for neighboring El Salvador in the 1970s. *Campesino* carries deeply positive meanings of the profound connection to the land (in its social, spiritual, and economic sense) and with the soil itself, from which life and sustenance is rooted for all.

Even when discussing ongoing land conflicts with me, people in Quezalte-peque talked in terms of "nosotros/ellos, los del pueblo" and "nosotros/ellos, los del campo los campesinos" (us/them from the town, us/them the rural people). These terms are particularly deployed in the conflicts between municipal administrators and the Comunidad de Indígenas over the custody of community lands.

Understanding the roots of these identities is key when interpreting the few stories that people shared with me about the Ten Years of Spring, stories about the control of community lands and those people who identify themselves as *naturales* and who see their roots linked to the Comunidad de Indígenas. Here are these stories.

Of Saints and Cattle

Each year the town ladinos would take their cattle to the *cumbre* (the mountain that divides the municipio of Quezaltepeque from that of Esquipulas) during the dry season, as these communal lands had the only viable pasture. This was a longstanding arrangement for which the ladino cattle owners paid a small fee to the Comunidad de Indígenas. However, in 1953, town residents found themselves trapped in their homes. The town was filled with cattle roaming up and down the cobbled streets, sometimes sticking their heads through wooden shutters and half doors. An old-timer recalled with laughter the foul smell and hazards of stepping out of the home those few days. Just imagine, he said to illustrate the scene, the surprised look of women who wanted to buy tortillas or take coffee to the mill and found a steer blocking their doors. He invited me to imagine the noise created when all those animals took over the streets.

A group of *campesino comuneros* (peasants with usufruct rights over the communal land) had herded the ladinos' cattle into town. The indigenous campesino leaders orchestrated the move to send a clear message to the town dwellers about control of the communal land. The Comunidad de Indígenas and the ladino-controlled municipality had a long history of disputes over the communal lands. In the midst of Arbenz's land reforms and growing political leverage of campesinos, the comuneros made their move, challenging the "tradition" that gave a group of powerful people unquestioned access to the communal pastures. The details of how long the negotiations took between the handful of powerful town ladinos and the comuneros, including exactly who was involved in solving the conflict, remain unclear. Today, communal land continues to feed the cattle of both *gente del pueblo* and *gente del campo,* and the conflicts over the administration of the land continue between the Comunidad de Indígenas and the municipality.

The second story also unfolds at the beginning of the dry season. November is the time for harvesting and for the local religious celebrations that honor San Francisco El Conquistador del Mundo. This San Francisco, with his own *cofradía* (religious brotherhood) house, contrasts with the town's official patron, San Francisco de Asís, housed in the main Roman Catholic Church. Two couples, of *padrinos* and *madrinas,* care for the saint and are considered the heads of all of the town's cofradías. Unlike the other *cofrades* (brothers), San Francisco's padrinos and madrinas manage their cofradía autonomously, not under the parish priest, and are considered priestly in some ways. The padrinos and madrinas are selected from the municipio's rural communities, and the rest of the cofradía members are recruited from outside the municipio. Those entering service must commit to two years of full-time work in town, leaving their homes and land in the care of others. Their obligations range from keeping the candles burning to directing all the agricultural rituals and giving special agricultural and healing advice. These people are thought of as quintessential Indians.

Quezaltepeque is no exception to the slow decline of Guatemala's cofradías. Yet, over the course of 1994, I witnessed a constant flow of visitors to San Francisco El Conquistador, and to the padrinos and madrinas. At the height of the saint's November fiesta, pilgrims formed long lines to his cofradía. People came from all over the region with offerings of food, money, and other material goods to pay their annual *promesa* (vow made to a saint in exchange for a favor).

On New Year's Eve 1994, San Francisco's padrinos, madrinas, and other cofrades worked all day and into the night, serving visitors *chilate* (corn gruel with cacao) and other special foods. They built an altar to receive people's offerings of flowers and vegetables. They and a select group of people that included ladinos and naturales spent days constructing one of Quezaltepeque's most important icons, El Torito Pinto. El Torito is a bull, handmade from reed mats, that is cattle-branded at San Francisco's cofradía. El Torito dances over a series of nights throughout the town's streets, paying homage to San Francisco El Conquistador on New Year's Eve. The dancing ends with *el amarre* (literally, "the tying up") on Epiphany, the sixth of January, when a padrino yokes and tames the bull.

On New Year's Eve, the office of padrinos and madrinas changes hands in *la pasada* (the passing). The new padrinos start the procession of San Francisco El Conquistador at the cofradía and run through the streets to the closed front doors of the town's church. Tradition holds that this San Francisco cannot enter the church. The midnight procession ends at the house where the new padrinos will live in town.

"It all changed when El Conquistador went to jail," stated a man, as a group of us waited for midnight and the beginning of the procession. Apparently, sometime in the 1950s—nobody seemed to remember exactly when—"the passing" of the saint ended in a stone-throwing fight. Witnesses explained that the outgoing padrinos had refused to pass the saint to the incoming padrinos and madrinas, who belonged to a different political party. The quarrel escalated, and the incoming padrinos attempted to force themselves into the saint's house. The eyewitnesses described the scene as total chaos, with stone throwing and machetes harming bystanders, pilgrims, and property. The police intervened, and to appease the mob, they put the saint behind bars until people settled down the next day.

And so ends the story of the saint who never entered a church, but did spend a night in jail. As a woman asked me, "Have you ever heard of a saint being taken to jail and never entering the church?" People frequently recounted the anecdote of the saint going to jail—but no one could remember exactly who did what, to whom, and when. The story's significance concerned not those details, but rather the framing of a time of change, of the opening of political parties and peasant organizations. Some told the story in approval, others in disapproval, of a saint who acted outside the command of the priests and the Catholic Church, and who had strong links to the local Comunidad de Indígenas and to the peasantry in the region, beyond the municipal boundaries.

Both stories, of the cattle in town and the saint in jail, illustrate a particular moment in which local identities and affiliations were at play. I first heard the story about the cattle descending into town from a town ladino. I asked many townspeople about it, but nobody else knew the story. When I interviewed several rural elders, on the other hand, they vividly confirmed, with much laughter, the incident.

People's selective memory and "silencing" of the details of the stories merit attention. I do not believe that the townspeople who lived through the Ten Years of Spring are "forgetting" the stories due to their insignificance. Instead, I believe that the stories are not told because these represent a time in which some *gente de campo* gained some power, some indigenous peasants even being democratically elected as mayors. Yet a few years after I heard pieces of these two stories, after the signing of the Peace Accords in 1996, I found that the grandchildren of the stories' protagonists were asking more questions about what had happened.

A New Political Era

In the months preceding the October Revolution, town dwellers and rural residents alike closely followed the news of the end of Ubico's regime. News spread through the radio, but even more so by word of mouth, from relatives and *paisanos* (compatriots or locals) living elsewhere. Residents lost no time in talking about the possibility of political changes, and preparing the political alliances between *la gente del pueblo* and *la gente del campo* that would later build the new political parties.[6]

People of Quezaltepeque were deeply divided either by their direct political affiliations or even their sympathy for the nascent political parties. Many indigenous peasants (and town dwellers) recounted feeling inspired by the policies that democratically elected President Arévalo promoted. Almost everyone remembered the political discourse of Arévalo's presidency as speaking to their highest values: equal opportunities for the peasantry and new opportunities for the rural ladinos, as well as a wider array of state jobs as health workers, educators, and construction workers.

Two of the indigenous mayors who served after the October Revolution explained that in the new political order, no matter how powerful a ladino was, he or she could not win an election without the campesino majority. Some argued in favor of recruiting indigenous leaders not just as mere followers but as candidates; the parties that ran indigenous leaders won elections. The rural people knew that to move forward their agendas, they had to get involved. Yet they had little or none of the political experience of the ladino town dwellers. It was a case of mutual dependency.

Local ladino politicians also played a key role in Quezaltpeque's progressive politics. Chiquimula's homegrown Leonardo Castillo Flores, who organized the Ligas Campesinas across Guatemala, was well remembered by one of the indigenous alcaldes I interviewed. Castillo Flores came in person to the milpas of Quezaltepeque to encourage peasants to organize. The alcalde described Castillo Flores as a *pobrecito* (literally, poor thing) referring to his humility and respectful manner. The alcalde also admired the ladinos of Guatemala City and Chiquimula who left behind their comforts to open the world of literacy for campesinos. Some campesinos, of which only a few survive today, took active roles in the so-called *mesas,* hamlet-size divisions of the Ligas Campesinas, particularly when the government of Arbenz launched his land reform decree. Peasants also organized themselves through a *unión campesina,* in great part with the help of Clodoveo Torres Moss, Quezaltepeque's "true" ladino, a lawyer who was a key figure during the Arbenz period.[7]

The ladinos' efforts paid off, as some indigenous peasants chose to ally with town ladinos from families that had long dominated local politics and economics. In sum, the ladinos needed the trust and the votes of the peasantry, and therefore chose their indigenous political partners carefully. The *naturales* saw in the ladinos a new window of political opportunities and mentorship, and they seized it. In the political dance that ensued, five indigenous mayors were elected to lead municipal politics.

Each of the three surviving indigenous alcaldes talked about the ways in which they tried to educate campesinos, particularly the unión campesina leaders, about Arbenz's agrarian reform. These men were able to recite word-for-word Decree 900 and felt betrayed by alarmist and fear-spreading rumors that divided people in Quezaltepeque. These rumors, about peasants threatening to take over ladino property—including land, households, even daughters—resonate with those documented by Jim Handy (1994) for other parts of the country. Interestingly, I learned about these rumors not from ladinos but from indigenous peasant leaders who looked back in despair at the ignorance, confusion, and politics of the time that ruined what they considered a fair and potentially fruitful project on land reform.

The day on which the cattle were driven from the mountain pastures into the town's main street is an example of the divisions. The new members of the unión campesina who also belonged to the Comunidad de Indígenas launched the battle over the custody of communal lands in the court.[8] The leaders of the unión campesina wanted to "stir up the issue" by organizing this event. They secured the cooperation of several campesinos and succeeded in sending much more than a symbolic message of their power: the ladinos might control more municipal and economic resources than the peasants, but if they had no access to the basic resources that feed their cattle, an important source of their wealth, they would have to cede their power to a peasant majority.

The last time I heard about the case, it turned on a complicated semantic point. One of the presidents of the Comunidad de Indígenas who served during the Arbenz period explained to me that the court dictated at that time that the land belonged to the *municipio* (township) of Quezaltepeque. This is not to be read as the *municipalidad,* one of the institutional bodies that administers the township. The colonial land title stipulates that the *naturales* and indios are the specific recipients of the royal title of the land, that is, the Comunidad de Indígenas. Comuneros pointed out that just because some members of the Comunidad de Indígenas organized themselves under the umbrella of a unión campesina back in the 1940s and 1950s, they did not have custody of the land title. The former institution, they insisted, had the historical weight and legitimacy that the latter organization did not have. Moreover, the comuneros asserted that the legitimacy of the uniones campesinas formed as legal bodies during the Arévalo and Arbenz presidencies ended when the Arbenz government was deposed.

The indigenous peasant majority, therefore, was divided as to how to achieve land reform. It is important to note that the department of Chiquimula had the largest number of organized *mesas* and yet the least land that could be affected by Decree 900 and the least number of actual expropriations in the whole country.[9]

Yes, there were differences among the campesinos, explained the surviving indigenous mayors. Yet these indigenous mayors felt strongly that they had prioritized the needs of the rural majority over those of the townspeople. They explained that, as indigenous alcaldes, they could talk to anyone as equals—which is not what a Castañeda, a Machón, or a Pinto (a few of the politically dominant ladino families) would do. Instead, the mayors and the people were all campesinos. They were all *naturales.*

Castillo Armas's *Entrada* and *La Liberación*

Whatever political power and openings the *naturales* gained between 1944 and 1954, these were cut off with Castillo Armas's army encampment in Quezaltepeque.

Compared to other places, Quezaltepeque did not suffer as much as other communities during the so-called "entrada de la liberación," in which Castillo Armas entered Guatemala with his U.S.-backed forces. As the opening story of this chapter recounts, the indigenous mayor of the time took brave and extraordinary measures to protect his people. He sent word to all political organizers to go into hiding immediately. He personally met the coup leader and instructed the town to provide hospitality to the invading army. He refused to provide names for the invaders' *listas negras*.

Stories that town dwellers tell about the immediate *entrada* range from statements such as "Here, there was only peace, because everyone quickly hung their white banners" to other statements from those who resented seeing their town center taken over by soldiers. The mayor's "hospitality" was a strategy to trick the colonel, and to "salvarse el cuello" (save his/her neck). Many *naturales,* men and women, were ordered to serve the invaders (i.e., wash their clothes, provide firewood, cook tortillas); among those serving, unbeknownst to the invaders, were allies of the *comunistas*. But even the mayor's strategy did not stop Castillo Armas from drawing up *listas negras* of Quezaltepeque people who had been active in Arbenz's political organizations.

In town, soldiers went house to house asking for the names of union organizers in Chiquimula or other political activists. The lists were already written, as the organizing had not been clandestine and had left a paper trail. In the rural areas, the lists included anyone who had received cows, machetes, and fertilizers through government programs. As a *natural* woman asked me rhetorically, "Who would have thought that the specially bred cow grazing in their backyard, a new breed they accepted in the hope of better feeding and clothing their family, would turn into a flag inviting death?"[10] Fifty years after this event, people still avoid offers "for free."[11]

By most accounts, only one resident, a campesino, was executed in Quezaltepeque. His death, however, is attributed to his refusal to heed the warnings from other campesinos to flee, including the indigenous mayor. Some remember him as one of the troublemakers and rumor mongers. However, no one, even those who did not share his views, felt he deserved execution.

The indigenous mayor who faced Castillo Armas explained to me that the political disputes between ladinos and government officials were not worth one drop of the campesinos' blood. He said, "Who was I to turn in the campesinos who were ignorant above all; who within this ignorance have fallen prey to other peoples' political games?" He also knew, instantly, that despite his ladino allies in the municipality, he was about to be the last indigenous mayor for a long time to come. And so it happened.

The extreme military repression to "clean the country" was unleashed first in the Oriente, led first by Castillo Armas (1954–57) and then by a series of colonel and generals. Carlos Manuel Arana Osorio, Guatemala's dictator from 1970 to 1974, was a leader in the 1954 Oriente's counterinsurgency campaign. The country's east became a source of military officials as well as other organizations and people that promoted control through violence and fear. The clandestine right-wing extremist Mano Blanca, a death squad, emerged from this part of the country and became conflated with the new, increasingly popular political party Movimiento de Liberacíon Nacional (MLN), which held control over much of the country's rural areas until the 1980s.[12] Members of this organization had access to arms (items typical of Oriente households) and built spy networks of individuals to identify and report suspects. In the neighboring towns of Esquipulas and Zacapa lived several ladino families that held great control over others through terror and violence. The stereotype of the wild lawless ladino east, in which matters are solved on an "eye for an eye, tooth for a tooth" basis, stood strong.

In Quezaltepeque, as in the rest of the Oriente, the dictatorships created new opportunities for certain people to taste the power that comes through the military.[13] Some ladinos played their role in the local military barracks at the top of the armies' hierarchies, while the *naturales* and the ladinos at the bottom of the social scale continued to serve at the bottom as forced recruits. Except now, their role was much more brutal. They were sent across the country to execute the terrors of the civil war in areas like the Verapaces, El Quiché, and El Petén.

In the aftermath, some leaders left, while others decided to return. Some residents welcomed the new order of political conservatism. Others went on with life as usual. But, with the silencing acts of terror either experienced or heard about in rumor by the community, the effervescent peasant political participation was cut short.

The silencing remains and deepens, fifty years after the end of the Arbenz government. People in the Oriente choose to "forget" to the point of actually forgetting what might have caused or might still cause the death of a family member, several generations later.[14] But I also note that, along with the silences, despite the fact that Quezaltepeque's residents have now developed into a conservative majority, at the time of the *entrada,* people did not betray each other, even across deep divisions of loyalty and interests. One day, during an interview, a self-proclaimed *natural campesino,* who was a leader in the local Liga Campesina, mused about how, not long before our talk, one of the most feared and conservative cacique ladinos of the MLN came up to him and said, "We are both now old. How is it that we both came to fight each other, and almost lost our lives in what turned out to be a pointless battle?" He ended the interview with me at that point, and after a long pause, looked away and invited me to see what he was working on when I showed up on his doorstep.

Notes

1. The ethnographic fieldwork includes visits in 1993, a long-term stay in 1994, and subsequent visits in 1997, 1998, 2000, and 2002.

2. This dichotomy is reflected in for example in the stellar works of Adams (1970) and MacLeod (1973), as well as Lutz and Lovell (1990). See the introduction chapters that summarize the state of the art of ethnographic research that focuses mostly on the Western Highlands in both Warren (1989) and Watanabe (1992 and 2000). For a post-1970s synthesis see Watanabe 2000. Beyond the now classic and historical works of Gillin (1943, 1951), Tumin (1950, 1952), and Wisdom (1940), this body of work in the Eastern Highlands is represented by Diener (1978), Durston (1972), Adams (1970: 217–223), and Kendall (1991). The Eastern Highlands have attracted a new wave of scholars in the 1990s and 2000s, and the area has become of great interest for scholars across disciplines. This body of work has been presented in conference papers, unpublished dissertations, and a few publications so far: Dary Fuentes (1995); Dary Fuentes, Elías, and Reina (1998); Little-Siebold (2006); López García and Metz (2002); Metz (1995, 2006); Moran-Taylor (2003); and Rodman (2006). The conference papers are not cited here.

3. See a more thorough discussion in Little-Siebold (2006).

4. See for instance Stavenhagen's (1962, 1969) often-quoted analysis in which he concludes that a class identity classification should be privileged to that of an ethnic identity classification to understand Guatemala's social relations. His description could not fit any more closely than what I found in Quezaltepeque, yet, based on what I observed there, one classification should not be privileged over the others as permanent abstract categories to explain social relations or the social landscape. Rather, these should be understood as intermeshed with each other. In the field it seems that one classification is more relevant than the other according to circumstances.

5. See Pearson (1969) on the important differences and functions that each of these levels of organization played in setting forth Arbenz's land reform.

6. In *Crucifixion by Power,* Adams (1970) notes the importance of noting the types of elites that operated in at least four cases studied: interregional, regional, and local. The typology comes particularly from Durston's (1972) research in Jutiapa in 1965.

7. For a couple of accounts on Torres Moss's role within the CNCG and the political parties see Handy (1994: 93, 104, 114–116).

8. The court documents and dictum are something that I have not examined up to this point. Here, however, the point I highlight is not what the resolution actually says but how this is being interpreted and used in the present day by both sides of the battle to claim legitimacy. On top of that, and regardless of the court resolution, what counts for the *comunero* (campesino that has usufruct rights over communal land) is the physical colonial land title, as conveyed in the phrase "tiene más poder que ningún otro papel!" (has more power than any other paper!).

9. This fact was brought to me by Todd Little-Siebold and his research notes at the INTA archive in March 2005. In Handy's (1994: 94) report about the actual number of expropriations, Chiquimula has the least number (three) of all the reported *departamentos* in the country.

10. There is some word that at a place called La Tigra there were people of Quezaltepeque who were executed and left half buried in a ditch. The victims are said to have been actively involved in the Liga Campesina while others were not, except that their names were listed in the records of the government development-type programs directed to agriculture. Almost everyone I asked about lives lost during "la liberación" says either that only one person had been killed or that lots of people were killed but are not sure that they were actually peasants from Quezaltepeque. This is still something up for careful questioning in the rural hamlets closer to Ipala, where I did not spent much time.

11. This subject of people shying from free offers usually came up in the context of political campaigns for presidential elections in which items like T-shirts and machetes are given away to peasants in the hope of buying their votes. The FRG campaigns, in which Alfonso Portillo Cabrera won the presidency, notably used this as a ploy to attract rural sympathizers and crowds to his public speeches.

12. See Adams (1970: 194–217).

13. For a succinct account of the period see Woodward, *A Short History of Guatemala* (2005: 127–153), and Handy, *Gift of the Devil: A History of Guatemala* (1984: 149–183).

14. See Carl Kendall (1991) on politics and religion in the pilgrimage site of the Basilica de Esquipulas. He was doing research there at a crucial and dangerous time in which Mano Blanca was particularly active. Unfortunately, he has not published more explicit information about the politics of the time there and his experiences elsewhere in the country, yet I was fortunate to learn a little bit about the Esquipulas of the time in a brief meeting with him in New Orleans in 1993.

Works Cited

Adams, Richard N.
  1970   Crucifixion by Power: Essays on Guatemalan National Social Structure, 1944–1966. Austin and London: University of Texas Press.

Dary Fuentes, Claudia
    1995   Entre el hogar y la vega: estudio sobre la participación femenina en la ag-
            ricultura de El Progreso. Guatemala: FLACSO.
Dary Fuentes, Claudia, Sílvel Elías, and Violeta Reina
    1998   Estrategias de sobrevivencia campesina en ecosistemas frágiles: los ch'orti'
            en las laderas secas del oriente de Guatemala. Guatemala: FLACSO.
Diener, Paul
    1978   The Tears of St. Anthony: Ritual and Revolution in Eastern Guatemala.
            Latin American Perspectives 5(3):92–116.
Durston, John W.
    1972   La estructura del poder en una región ladina de Guatemala. El Depar-
            tamento de Jutiapa. Guatemala: Seminario de Integración Social Guate-
            malteca. Estudios Centoramericanos 7.
Gillin, John Philip
    1943   Houses, Food, and the Contact of Cultures in a Guatemalan Town. Acta
            Americana 1:344–359.
    1951   The Culture of Security in San Carlos. A Study of a Guatemalan Community
            of Indians and Ladinos. New Orleans: Tulane University, Middle American
            Research Institute, publication 16.
Handy, Jim
    1984   Gift of the Devil: A History of Guatemala. Boston: South End Press.
    1994   Revolution in the Countryside: Rural Conflict and Agrarian Reform in
            Guatemala, 1944–1954. Chapel Hill: University of North Carolina Press.
Kendall, Carl
    1991   The Politics of Pilgrimage: The Black Christ of Esquipulas. In Pilgrimage
            in Latin America. N. Ross Crumrine and Alan Morines, eds. Pp. 139–156.
            New York: Greenwood Press.
Little Siebold, Christa
    2006   "En La Tierra de San Francisco El Conquistador: Identity, Faith, and Liveli-
            hood in Quezaltepeque, Chiquimula." Ph.D. dissertation, Department of
            Anthropology, Tulane University, New Orleans.
López García, Julián, and Brent E. Metz
    2002   Primero Dios. Etnografía y cambio social entre los mayas ch'orti's del oriente
            de Guatemala. Guatemala: FLACSO.
Lutz, Christopher H., and George W. Lovell
    1990   Core and Periphery in Colonial Guatemala. In Guatemalan Indians and
            the State, 1540–1988. Carol A. Smith, ed. Pp. 35–51. Austin: University of
            Texas Press.
MacLeod, Murdo J.
    1973   Spanish Central America: A Socioeconomic History, 1520–1720. Berkeley:
            University of California Press.
Maxwell, Judith M.
    1982   Nahual-pipil: muy político. Cultural Survival Quarterly 6(1):17–18.

Metz, Brent
   1995   Experiencing Conquest: The Political and Economic Roots and Cultural Expression of Maya-Chorti Ethos. PhD. dissertation, Department of Anthropology, University at Albany, State University of New York.
   2006   Ch'orti'-Maya Survival in Eastern Guatemala: Indigeneity in Transition. Albuquerque: University of New Mexico Press.
Moran-Taylor, Michelle
   2003   International Migration and Culture Change in Guatemala's Maya Occidente and Ladino Oriente. Ph.D. dissertation, Department of Anthropology, Arizona State University.
Oakes, Maud
   1951   The Two Crosses of Todos Santos. Survivals of Mayan Religious Ritual. New York: Bollingen Foundation.
Pearson, Neale J.
   1969   Guatemala: The Peasant Union Movement, 1944–1954. *In* Latin American Peasant Movements. Henry Landsberger, ed. Ithaca, N.Y.: Cornell.
Rodman, Debra H.
   2006   Gender, Migration, and Transnational Identity: Maya and Ladino Relations in Eastern Guatemala. Ph.D. dissertation, Department of Anthropology, University of Florida.
Stavenhagen, Rodolfo
   1962   Estratificación social y estructura de clases. Ciencias Politicas y Sociales 27:73–102.
   1969   Las clases sociales en las sociedades agrarias. México: Siglo XXI.
Tumin, Melvin
   1950   The Dynamics of Cultural Discontinuity in a Peasant Society. Social Forces 29:135–141.
   1952   Caste in a Peasant Society. Princeton, N.J.: Princeton University Press.
Warren, Kay B.
   1989[1978]   The Symbolism of Subordination: Indian Identity in a Guatemalan Town. Austin: University of Texas Press.
Watanabe, John M.
   1992   Maya Saints and Souls in a Changing World. Austin: University of Texas Press.
   2000   Maya and Anthropologists in the Highlands of Guatemala since the 1960's. *In* Supplement to the Handbook of Middle American Indians. Volume 6. Pp. 224–247. Austin: University of Texas Press.
Wisdom, Charles
   1940   The Chorti Indians of Guatemala. Chicago: University of Chicago Press.
Woodward, Ralph Lee, Jr.
   2005   A Short History of Guatemala. Guatemala: Editorial Laura Lee.

5

The Path Back to Literacy

Maya Education through War and Beyond

JUDITH M. MAXWELL

Before Guatemala's democratic "spring" there was the "winter" of Ubico's content. What did this mean in terms of education? President Jorge Ubico y Castañeda supported increased education for the indigenous population and decreed that bilingual education should be available in rural areas. His 1938 decree classified the areas and townships of Guatemala as either "urban" or "rural." This became the basis for allocating funds for social and educational projects, assigning teachers, and delivering services. The classification remains operative despite massive population shifts. Ubico made finca owners responsible for providing schools should their farms have ten or more school-age children in residence. He stipulated that a major goal of the schools was to teach Spanish, the national language. In 1938 he established a national agricultural secondary school, giving five years of agronomy training for grade-school graduates. The national normal school he established trained indigenous teachers until his ouster. Military training had been part of the grade-school curriculum since Manuel Estrada Cabrera's administration (1898–1920). Ubico expanded the curriculum, adding weapons drills and parades for secondary schools. He established military courses with officers as the designated instructors as a requisite part of secondary education, Article 2201. Each year of secondary-school study awarded a different military rank, from corporal through first sergeant. Graduates of normal schools received a lieutenant's rank along with their teaching credentials. The autonomy of the national university was revoked. Military personnel were charged with the university administration. Student associations were banned, until pressure from the United States for increased democracy led Ubico to legalize student unions. Students (primarily university level) and teachers (from throughout the country, but most heavily from the capital) sought to break Ubico's control. June 30 has long been Teachers Day in Guatemala. This holiday is marked by teachers parading and being honored by their communities. In 1944 on June 29 rather than parade as usual, the teachers took to the streets in protest. Students joined them, amassing the largest street demonstration in Guatemala's history. Ubico called out the military, and in the violence that ensued two hundred people were killed or wounded. María Chinchilla, a leader of the teacher's union, became a martyr to the cause. Ubico lost control in the increasing unrest and was almost immediately deposed by a military coup, which then rushed to elections, elections that brought in the Diez Años de Primavera (Ten Years of Spring).

Juan José Arévalo Bermejo, president of Guatemala from 1945 to 1951, was an educator. He received his degree as a primary-school teacher in 1922. His first book was *Método nacional para aprender simultáneamente dibujo, escritura y lectura*. In 1934 he received a doctorate in education from the Universidad de La Plata, in Buenos Aires, Argentina. He left his position as a professor at the Universidad de Tucumán in 1944 to launch his presidential campaign. Once elected, he set about improving the national educational system. The revolutionary junta of 1944 had established the autonomy of the Universidad de San Carlos, the national university. In September 1945 Arévalo launched the Humanities Faculty there. This faculty included the disciplines of philosophy, letters, history, and pedagogy. Arévalo was also responsible for adding psychology and journalism as major fields. He founded the Institute of Anthropology and History and the Instituto Indigenista Nacional (IIN). He expanded secondary education, creating new secondary schools in the capital and in the countryside. In 1949 he developed a new type of school, the "federation" school. In these schools each classroom would set its own educational goals and plans of study, sharing a library, sports, audiovisual facilities, and administration with other classrooms. Through his newly founded Departamento de Educación Rural, he established six thousand federal schools, most in rural areas previously unserved. Adding to the traditional curriculum of the grade schools, Arévalo insisted on instruction in agronomy, industrial arts, and vocational training. He expanded the budget for the Ministry of Education publishing arm, so it could produce more textbooks and teaching materials, which were then distributed to remote as well as city schools. Arévalo also established a teacher rank and pay scale that has served the Ministry of Education ever since. He set up child day-care centers where preschooling would be available. In addition to classroom schooling, Arévalo launched a massive literacy campaign. He established bilingual education programs in the four *lenguas mayoritarias* (majority languages; K'ichee', Kaqchikel, Mam, and Q'eqchi'). He reached out to rural communities through a mobile cultural mission that was supposed to help isolated settlements lacking regular schools. The educational materials did not employ the term *indígena,* instead characterizing all rural Guatemalans as *campesinos.* The cultural programming of the mobile mission was evangelizing the good news of modernization, with indigenous practices and values explicitly labeled *ignorantes.* In Arévalo's last term of office, the education budget constituted the largest single item of public finance.

Jacobo Arbenz tried to establish an income tax, with a watered-down version passed three years into his term. Because his main platform was agrarian reform, not much further attention was paid to educational reform, though money from the income tax was allotted to keep the rural schools established by Arévalo operating. The Ministry of Education, nonetheless, continued its policy of preferentially giving posts, including rural "bilingual" positions, to ladino graduates with teaching certificates, regardless of their fluency in the local language.

It should be stressed that the principal aim of education in the postcoup "winter" as well as the democratic "spring" was assimilation of the indigenous population into the "national" culture. The stress on Spanish as a unifying language that had begun under colonial rule was continued in the republic. The 1842 legislative decree 14 affirms that

> the constituent Congress of the Guatemalan State, considering that there should be *one* national language, and while those [languages] that the first indigenes still conserve are not [held in] common nor are equal to the task of illuminating the people, nor perfecting civilization in that sizeable portion of the State, has seen fit to decree:
>
> > (1) The parochial priests, in conjunction with the municipal authorities of the towns will procure through the most fitting, prudent, and efficient means, to extinguish the language of the first indigenes. (reprinted in Skinner-Klee 1954)

In 1879 primary-school education was made compulsory and free, though no provisions were made for schools to provide for six years of primary instruction in all communities. In 1921 the constitution of the short-lived Central American Republic reaffirmed the principle of compulsory and free lay primary-school education. In 1929 rural centers were established under the rubric *escuelas de castellanización.* Their goal was to teach the indigenous population to speak and understand Spanish, and to read (and sign) documents.

Bilingual Education and a New Orthography

In 1945 Guatemala wrote a new constitution of its own. Article 4 established Spanish as the sole official language. In 1946 the Law of Governance and Administration of the Departments of the Republic declared that the indigenous population should be "incorporated," but stipulated that this incorporation should respect "their customs, religious creeds and language" (Congreso 1946). The 1956 constitution again affirms the role of Spanish as the sole national language. In 1964 the Dirección de Desarrollo Socio-Educativo Rural was established, replacing the rural programs of the *escuelas de castellanización.* The Guatemalan constitution was revised in 1965, again declaring Spanish official. This document spells out the role of education in the development of the citizens' physical and spiritual well-being and in article 96 posits literacy as a matter for urgent national attention. The Organic Education Act, also of 1965, established bilingual education in the big four indigenous languages, K'ichee', Mam, Kaqchikel, and Q'eqchi.' The goal of this education was again assimilatory. The indigenous language was to be used to facilitate the transition to literacy in Spanish. In 1976 legislative decree 73-76 (Congreso 1976) reiterated the compulsory nature of primary-school education, but with the stipulation that both the education provided and the enculturation should be in both the official language and "lenguas indígenas." In 1978 the literacy law was passed, declaring that illiterate persons between the ages of fifteen and forty-five should receive training in reading, writing, and arithmetic. Several articles of this law considered the use of indigenous languages, but always as a bridge to Spanish. An individual was to be deemed literate when she or he could participate in the *cultura nacional,* which entailed being able to read, write, and do sums (within the decimal system, rather than the Maya vigesimal system). The National Education Act of 1977 specified that "*castellanización* is an educational process that tries to give the indigenous population the knowledge necessary for the comprehension and the utilization of the Spanish language, with the goal of facilitating their communication and co-living (*convivencia*) within the country" (Congreso 1977).

In 1982 the government established the Programa Nacional de Educación Bilingüe (PRONEBI). This was deemed an experimental program to try "true" bilingual education. Once again the big four indigenous languages, known by the epithet *idiomas mayoritarios,* were targeted. Sam Colop (1983), Maya intellectual, writing his licenciatura thesis scarcely a year after the establishment of PRONEBI, found this new organ of the Ministry of Education no different in its assimilationism. Demetrio Cojtí Cuxil (1987, 1989, 1994), who earned his doctorate in Belgium and later became head of UNICEF Guatemala and vice minister of education for Guatemala, broadly categorized all Ministry of Education programs in Maya areas as assimilationist, accusing the ministry of cultural genocide. However, workers within PRONEBI believed they had another agenda. They worked feverishly to produce elementary-school textbooks with Maya content. Artists sought to represent the *traje* (native dress) and towns of the areas in which the books were to be used, while constrained by the need to produce images that could be copied across four major language groups. Consulting with the Mam and Kaqchikel teams working on content, I learned that math was a particular concern. They were trying to develop ways to teach math in base twenty—which is what the Maya system uses—while allowing for an eventual transition to or addition of decimal and binary systems. The materials were developed one year and grade level at a time. The initial program was envisioned as lasting through grade four with gradual increase of Spanish language curriculum, so that by grade five the student would be in an all–Spanish language environment, or possibly one in which the indigenous language became a fifth subject, after *idioma* ("language," though only Spanish language was taught), social sciences, natural sciences, and mathematics. "After" often meant in class times outside normal school times. The initial pilot with the *idiomas mayoritarios* was deemed a success. Children in the bilingual classes were performing at or above the level of children in traditional monolingual classrooms. In 1984 PRONEBI was expanded to include four more languages—Q'anjob'al, Ixil, Poqomchi', and Tz'utujil—with only some thirteen language groups remaining outside the bilingual education system. Because the program was minimally funded, no further coverage was contemplated.

The path of implementation of PRONEBI was rocky. Some of the largest obstacles were parental resistance, lack of trained teachers, and language standardization in textbooks. Parents were often not pleased to find their children being instructed in the indigenous language. Having suffered discrimination themselves, recalling their experiences in school when faced with a monolingual, Spanish-speaking teacher who typically did not allow the indigenous language to be spoken on the school grounds, and believing that job advancement required Spanish fluency and literacy, the parents did not want their children "held back" by their native language. Indeed, many parents had refused to pass on the indigenous language to their children, so the children were functionally monolingual in Spanish, with passive to no competence in the indigenous language. The parents then felt their children would be at a disadvantage in a bilingual classroom, especially one that was almost monolingual in the native tongue for the first grade. In addition, they felt that time spent on teaching the indigenous language would be better spent on math or arts. This feeling was largely echoed by the teachers.

Programs were hampered by the composition of the teaching staff of most rural schools. The teachers tended to be ladinos. When indigenous teachers had been placed in government teaching posts, they were usually placed in communities with a different language to insure that they would not speak to the children in a language other than Spanish. With bilingual education the new goal, the lack of teachers with appropriate language skills became problematic. PRONEBI was able to place some bilingual teachers in understaffed schools. But even these teachers often did not follow the draft curriculum. They tended to use the newly developed textbooks for a few weeks and then transition to the more familiar Spanish-language materials and methods. In 1987 PRONEBI countered by establishing roving inspections. Supervisors were provided with motorcycles to make the circuit of the rural schools unannounced to ensure that teachers and children were interacting in the appropriate indigenous language and using PRONEBI materials. One such inspector, Wuqub' Ajpub', confided to me that he found Spanish being used almost exclusively in his first years as an inspector. After four years, in 1991 just before he switched to a job in the capital, he found only about 20 percent compliance. These figures were confirmed by another inspector, Kaqb'alam.

Let me break from the narrative of governmental actions a moment to broaden the discussion. By the early 1980s, several governmental organizations were charged with educating Mayas, teaching them to read and write and to speak Spanish. Operating at this time we had some old *escuelas de castellanización* superseded, but not replaced by Socio-educativo Rural. These groups were explicitly charged with teaching Spanish and developing Spanish literacy. Both had begun to use indigenous languages as a bridge. Individual workers were creatively developing writing systems to represent the indigenous languages. Meanwhile, the Summer Institute of Linguistics (SIL), founded in 1934 by William Cameron Townsend, had a strong presence in Guatemala. Townsend himself had worked in Kaqchikel communities, had developed a writing system for the language, and had published studies of the verbal system. He had also expanded his studies to other Mayan languages of Guatemala. SIL expanded as well, bringing in scholars to work in Maya communities throughout Guatemala. These workers were encouraged to write phonemically and in the manner of the people within the community, so that two varieties of K'ichee' might be represented with differing, though similar orthographies, local realizations being of paramount importance. In 1952 SIL became an advisory organization to the government on indigenous language issues. The publishing arm of SIL thereby gained semigovernmental standing, with the result that the Mayan alphabet as written by SIL was de facto officialized.

In 1969 a group of friars had charged Robert Gersony with bringing to fruition their dream of an indigenous-language teaching institute, dedicated to teaching indigenous people about and in their own languages. Gersony formed a lay institution with initial international financing through Oxfam and support from the U.S. Peace Corps, and forged an uneasy alliance with the Ministry of Education. This institute was dubbed the Proyecto Lingüístico Francisco Marroquín (PLFM), which trains indigenous linguists, publishes works in and on Mayan languages, and supports itself by teaching Spanish, and occasionally a Mayan language, to foreigners. The PLFM, in turn, developed its own Mayan alphabet, or series of alphabets, as it expanded its coverage from three to eight and eventually seventeen languages.

In 1959 the K'ichee' scholar Adrián Inez Chávez organized the K'ichee' intellectual community in and around Xelajub' No'j (Quetzaltenango) to form the Academia de la Lengua Maya Kí-chè. He developed an orthography, at once more iconic and less Latinate, including * for [ch'] as the initial sound of *ch'umiil* (star), and ☀ for [q'] as the initial sound of *q'iij* (day, sun). A cooperative of K'ichee' authors and artisans soon formed and used this alphabet or adaptations thereof.

Another alphabet in the mix was the colonial (Roman) alphabet and adaptations thereof. The Franciscan priest Fray Francisco de la Parra had developed a Latin-based alphabet with additional symbols to represent the postvelar and glottalized consonants of the Mayan languages. Indigenous scribes were trained in the use of this alphabet, as well as originally being taught Latin and Spanish. Though the Spanish court soon opted for preferential use of Nahuatl as the indigenous language for proselytization and for official documents, wills, land titles, town records, and the like continued to be written in Mayan languages for many years. Some of these documents were kept by leading families, who had some familiarity with the writing, though by the end of the sixteenth century the value of the special de la Parra symbols had largely been forgotten.

By the early 1980s, there were numerous alphabets in use. Though these alphabets tended to differ by only a small subset of symbols (between eight and thirteen), these inconsistencies frustrated newly literate and semiliterate speakers and writers. The multiplicity of alphabets, even those produced by governmental and semigovernmental agencies, made it difficult for the government to produce official communications in indigenous languages. In response to this need and to the clamor of teachers working for literacy projects as well as in PRONEBI schools, the government called for a national conference on the alphabets used for indigenous languages. The Segundo Congreso sobre el Alfabeto, held in 1984, included delegates from all the major organizations producing pedagogical materials in the Mayan languages of Guatemala. There was an open invitation to all interested people to participate. Everyone, whether a member of an invited organization or an independent agent, was allowed to address the assembly. However, only the indigenous participants were allowed to vote. A new alphabet emerged from the assembly, one strikingly like the PLFM alphabet, with the exception of using 7 to represent glottal stop. Moreover, the conference ratified principles for determining what an orthography should be like: one symbol per phoneme, characters easily represented by symbols found on a standard Latin American typewriter or computer keyboard. They explicitly rejected similarity to Spanish spelling conventions and its correlate, easy transference to Spanish, as criteria.

Another unprogrammed outcome of this conference was a cadre of Mayan linguists (largely alumni of the PLFM), educators, and activists agreed to remain "convened" as an "academy" for the promotion of Mayan languages. Their first order of business was to lobby for official recognition as the body in charge of Mayan languages, Mayan writing practices, literacy, and education.

Meanwhile, the PLFM continued to bring in small cohorts of willing Maya students not only to learn to read and write in their languages, but also to learn linguistic principles and to apply these to the study of the autochthonous languages. In 1975 the PLFM had hosted the first Taller de Lingüística Maya at what was then its main campus, the Rancho Nimajay. Representatives from the SIL, scholars from the United States, and PLFM students participated, giving professional papers, sharing data, and comparing notes in break-out discussions. This meeting was so successful that it was decided to be repeated annually. At the second workshop in 1976, Robert Laughlin's group of puppeteers and teachers from Chiapas participated, making the meetings Pan-Mayan. The third meeting was hosted by the Universidad Autónoma de Yucatán in Mérida, Mexico. However, the lack of participation by native speakers of Yucateco and the cost of travel to Mexico for the Guatemalans, the majority of the exponents, led to the resolution to hold successive meetings in Guatemala. The fourth workshop was held in Cobán. By this time, these linguistic fora had begun to attract the attention of Mayas interested in their languages, especially in Mayan language pedagogy, though the program was still academic. Papers ranged from ergative marking to the interaction of topicalization and subordination. In response to feedback from the attendees at this workshop, the following workshop began with a two-day crash course in linguistic principles, with special attention given to principles for establishing practical orthographies. This fifth Taller de Lingüística Maya was held in Sololá. Panels addressed questions of pedagogy; workers for Socio-Educativo Rural, teachers at local schools, and individuals with private nongovernmental organizations (NGOs) reported on their writing practices and their neologisms. However, the "straight" linguists began to feel that real scholarship was being buried by these applied concerns. A sixth workshop was held in 1980 at the Universidad Rafael Landívar. Here the papers were almost purely research oriented. Fewer Mayas from rural schools attended, and representatives of PRONEBI came for their own presentations but did not hear anyone else's presentations. This sixth workshop demonstrated that another means of sharing information was needed, so in 1997 the workshop was superseded by the Congreso de Estudios Mayas, a scholarly conference including but not limited to linguistic and language pedagogy issues.

Meanwhile, in 1985 a new federal constitution had been drafted. This constitution once again asserted the primacy of Spanish as the official language and that which defined national culture. However, indigenous languages were acknowledged as part of the national patrimony, and rights to continue to use them and to participate in indigenous cultural practices were affirmed. So, although still placing indigenous languages and cultures on a second tier, this document did affirm their right to exist and their importance to the country as part of national identity.

A Consensus on Alphabets

In 1987 the Guatemalan congress passed governmental accord 1046-87, which established a new "unified" orthography for the Mayan languages of Guatemala. This was essentially a ratification of the findings of the 1984 Segundo Congreso sobre el Alfabeto. But it also officially recognized twenty-one Mayan languages, detailing the specific symbols used to represent phonemes in each. Also that year, the Guatemalan congress established the Academia de las Lenguas Mayas de Guatemala (ALMG). The cohort of scholars formed at the alphabet conference were the core of this new semiautonomous organ of the government. They quickly established a governing council and sought representation of the twenty-one linguistic communities. They came under attack almost immediately for not doing enough to promote Mayan languages, for not moving against those who did not use the newly official alphabet, and for not immediately producing materials for all the indigenous languages. However, the ALMG proceeded slowly, spending most of the first year in establishing a grassroots (or tree roots, since one of their early projects involved planting trees) base. The law did not provide a means of censoring or censuring those who did not abide by the new consensus on alphabets. The ALMG simply sought to promote the use of Mayan languages in public domains; it was influential in getting news media, particularly *Siglo XXI,* to run features in Mayan languages.

Also in 1987, the Universidad Rafael Landívar began a program to prepare Mayas for professional careers, particularly in law and medicine; the Programa para el Desarrollo Integral de la Población Maya (PRODIPMA) was run primarily from the Quetzaltenango campus. The initial years were difficult. The teaching staff were ladinos, many of whom had not taught indigenous students before. I was called in by the vice rector, Guillermina Hernández, to ascertain why nearly all the Maya students were flunking. The instructors identified written work as the key problem. They claimed Mayas did not know how to write and that the essays were repetitive and vague. Upon reviewing examples, it became clear that Mayas had imported their own literary canons, including parallelism, couplet structure, and semantic bracketing for key ideas. Hernández held workshops for the *catedráticos* to sensitize them to Mayan literary tropes, as well as workshops for the students on academic writing practices. After the initial years, confrontations over academic style abated, but charges of misuse of scholarship funds arose. Many Mayas claimed that few Maya students could participate in the Maya educational program because the scholarships were awarded only to ladinos with connections to university officials. Eventually, the mechanisms for awarding the scholarships were redefined, with control switching to the central campus in many cases.

Meanwhile, back at the Ministry of Education, reform was underway again. Governmental accord 470-89 was enacted in July 1989. This formed a new division within the ministry: Sistema Integral de Mejoramiento y Adecuación Curricular (SIMAC). Two of the top four scholars on the SIMAC board were Mayas. They envisioned a Freireian educational system, where the local communities, parents, teachers, and students all worked together to determine what the curriculum would be for a given year. This led to a great deal of variation in implementation and at times "orders" from the central administration that seemed contradictory, leading to frustration at the local level and refusal by some schools to even open books supplied by SIMAC.

In 1990 ALMG's work was affirmed by governmental decree 65-90, which made the academy an autonomous governmental institution, increasing the dedicated funds and licensing radio broadcasts.

In the same year the U.S. Agency for International Development (USAID) sponsored a Basic Education Strengthening (BEST) program to enhance elementary education, beginning with a massive dialect survey. Its goals were to determine dialect variants as well as to identify communities in which more than one language was spoken, so multiple educational texts could be developed and provided. BEST ran until 1997.

In 1991 the Comisión Consultiva de Reforma Educativa was established to explore strategies for increasing the number of Maya girls entering school and then to enhance their chances of completing elementary and even secondary education. This commission established the Programa de Educación de la Niña, which, along with the Instituto Lingüístico of Universidad Rafael Landívar, began a campaign to change attitudes toward educating girls. The government wanted to promote smaller families, particularly in rural areas, and stressed that girls who stayed in school delayed starting families. Other values touted were students' ability to get better-paid jobs, and increased access to government services. USAID funded the publication of a short story in booklet format, *Ri k'ayewal xuk'owisaj ri ch'uti Manuelita* (The troubles of Manuelita), which was translated into eight Mayan languages and Spanish. The book tells of the trials Manuelita and her family overcome so that she can go to school and get an education.

In 1992 Celestino Alfredo Tay Coyoy became the first Maya minister of education. Under his leadership, a program of bootstrapping Mayan-language community schools, Escuelas Mayas, was established. Though this program did not survive Tay Coyoy's tenure, literally hundreds of community-operated and -financed elementary schools—in which instruction was primarily in Mayan languages, with little or no Spanish training as part of the curriculum—came into existence. Most have managed to survive even without government subvention. Given oversight of the Maya schools, CEDIM (Centro de Documentación e Investigación Maya) continues to build library resources and to provide training programs for Maya educators as well as for researchers and scholars.

By the early 1990s the number of Maya educational institutions had grown. Though some are partially overseen or sponsored by the Ministry of Education, most are not. The Consejo Nacional de Educación Maya (CNEM) was formed in 1993 to coordinate educational philosophy and to suggest methodologies for culturally sensitive pedagogy. The following institutions were founding members of CNEM:

- Academia de las Lenguas Mayas de Guatemala (ALMG), Guatemala City
- Asociación Científica y Cultural (Xeljú), Quetzaltenango
- Asociación de Centros Educativos Mayas de Nivel Medio (ACEM), Guatemala City
- Asociación de Estudio, Investigación y Promoción de la Cultura Maya (Ub'eal Tzij), Santo Domingo Xenacoj, Sacatepéquez
- Asociación de Escuelas Mayas de Nivel Primario, El Estor, Izabal
- Asociación de Educadores Bilingües Q'eqchi' de Izabal (ADEBQ'I), Izabal
- Asociación de Padres de Familia, Santo Domingo Xenacoj, Sacatepéquez
- Asociación la Huella del Varón de Rabinal Achí, Cobán, Alta Verapáz
- Asociación para el Desarrollo de la Comunidad Guatemalteca (ADECOGUA), Chimaltenango
- Asociación Regional de Mujeres Mayas del Norte, Cobán, Alta Verapáz
- Centro de Documentación e Investigación Maya (CEDIM), Guatemala City
- Centro de Estudios de la Cultura Maya (CECMA), Guatemala City
- Consejo Maya (Jun Ajpu Ixb'alamke), Guatemala City
- Cooperación para el Desarrollo Rural de Occidente (CDRO), Totonicapán
- Dirección General de Educación Bilingüe Intercultural (DIGEBI) del Ministerio de Educación, Guatemala City
- Fundación Rigoberta Menchú Tum, Guatemala City
- Instituto La Salle de Santa María Visitación, Sololá
- Movimiento Nacional (Uk'ux Mayab' Tinimit), Guatemala City
- Programa de Desarrollo Económico y Social de la Mujer (Kichin Konojel), Chimaltenango
- Proyecto de Desarrollo Santiago (PRODESSA), Guatemala City
- Sociedad El Adelanto, Quetzaltenango
  (http://www.guate.net/cnem/plan.html, accessed April 3, 2004)

By 1995 the peace process brought about the signing of part 3 of the Acuerdos de Paz: the Agreement on Indigenous Peoples' Identity and Rights. This docu-

ment affirmed that indigenous people had a right to education in their autochthonous languages and with Maya cultural norms, not just through three
years of elementary schooling but through the university level. It did not state
that transition to Spanish language was an obligatory or even a desirable end.
Moreover, the Accord stated that, provided the indigenous peoples so desired,
one or more indigenous languages might be made co-official with Spanish.

Also in 1995, governmental accord 726-95 established the right of indigenous girls to education and initiated the Programa de la Niña under the
supervision of SIMAC. The goals of this program were to encourage girls to
continue their studies through professional or vocational career programs
and to help place them in positions. Other explicit goals included the raising of healthier children through improved living conditions, training in
proper nutrition and education for their children, and limiting the number
of offspring *adecuado a sus posibilidades* (according to the mothers' circumstances). By 1997 this program had become the Seminario Nacional de
Educación de la Niña, with U.N. sponsorship.

Governmental decree 726-95 transformed PRONEBI into the Dirección
General de Educación Bilingüe Intercultural (DIGEBI). Mayas working for
the Ministry of Education considered this name change more than cosmetic.
They interpreted it as an acknowledgment of the necessity to include indigenous people not just as a stopgap or transition but as a permanent part of
the national educational enterprise. They saw themselves as being placed on
a more equal footing with ladino colleagues. Moreover, the mission was no
longer simply bilingual education, but bilingual intercultural education. The
Ministry of Education was paying serious attention to the pluriculturality of
the nation.

Expanding and Normalizing Mayan Languages

I was invited in 1995 to participate in a neologisms project sponsored by
the ALMG. Working primarily with Kaqchikel Cholchi' but in consultation with seven other linguistic communities, we devised for the national
curriculum new Mayan words needed in grades one through four. These
words fell under the rubrics of the standard Spanish-language schools: language, social science, natural science, and math. However, care was taken
not merely to provide translation for Spanish concepts, but to provide vocabulary that would allow Maya categories in these domains to be readily
expressed. Thus, "language" vocabulary included not only the noun, verb,
adjective, and prepositional word classes of Spanish (and English), but also

ergative, absolutive, relational noun, and positional. Rules were devised for proposing new terms: the rules of the Mayan languages were to be strictly respected at all levels, from phonology through pragmatics; terms should be lexemes rather than descriptions (or, as Ixcha'im put it, "no *kilométricos*"); where possible archaic terms should be retaken with appropriate semantic adjustment; languages within a linguistic group should select forms with a shared cognate root and/or set of derivations when possible as the bases for building the new word. Once the words were proposed, they were submitted to panels of teachers and community leaders. Where the derivations were not transparent, some discussion of the reasoning behind the suggestions was required. The archaic forms, though often unrecognized and therefore questioned, always met with approval. Neologisms made by building roots that filled phonological gaps were less well-received. If a root with a related semantic field could be found, panelists preferred to stretch its domain rather than bring in wholly novel forms. When the referent was a new product, the new roots were more easily approved. Forms that were derived by regular morphological processes were more popular than forms that utilized less productive affixes. All forms were cycled through the proposal-feedback-ratification loop at least twice before being forwarded to the U.N. Children's Fund (UNICEF), the funding agency, and published. These publications were distributed to the participating ALMG regional offices, but most communities failed to systematically utilize them or provide local schools and teachers with working copies. In 1997 came a brief resurgence in the self-generated schools. The administrators of this initiative were reassigned during Alfonso Portillo Cabrera's presidency, and the initiative again lapsed.

In 1998 Edumaya was launched with funding from USAID and Universidad Rafael Landívar. Edumaya was a professionalization program, replacing the earlier Landívar initiative PRODIPMA. Speakers of Mayan languages were to be trained as teachers, writers, and interpreters. Special programs in court interpretation were inaugurated pursuant to the 1995 Peace Accords provision for court proceedings to be translated into Mayan languages when Mayas were present as defendants or plaintiffs.

The Consulta Popular in May 1999 was expected to ratify mechanisms for enacting legislation mandated by the Peace Accords. The resounding defeat of this referendum stunned many Maya educators and scholars, who were poised to expand their efforts in promoting Mayan language use. Weeks of analysis and caucusing resulted in a resolve to continue with their plans to implement new initiatives, relying on the Peace Accords per se as well as other international agreements to which Guatemala was a party, including the Indigenous and Tribal Peoples Convention (ILO-Convention 169) and the Universal Declaration of Human Rights.

Despite worries that Alfonso Portillo, who became president in 2000, might enact policies detrimental to indigenous education, he instead pushed through a new federal budget that allowed the Ministry of Education to meet the goals for expanding all education and bilingual education in particular. In the following year, the general education budget did not expand, as military spending cuts did not follow the guidelines projected in the Peace Accords, but bilingual education held its own and even slightly expanded. Self-generated school spending was phased out, and Maya schools were encouraged to join the national system, though many chose to remain under CNEM and CEDIM sponsorship.

Tay Coyoy was replaced as minister of education by a non-Indian, Mario Torres. However, Dr. Waqi' Q'anil Cojtí Cuxil became the vice minister. Some indigenous teachers and scholars within the government and the ministry as well as in independent NGOs hoped that Cojtí would place even more emphasis on bilingual education, as he had been a strong advocate of bilingual education research and materials development in his position as head of UNICEF in Guatemala. While giving strong support to the existing programs, Cojtí did not lobby for a great shift in resource allocation; he observed that he had been appointed vice minister of education for all of Guatemala, not just for Mayas.

Nonetheless, in 2002 the Ministry of Education opened seventeen normal schools for bilingual education. In 2003 an additional seven normal schools had been opened. Indigenous normal school graduates of these institutions and of older Indian schools were given government teaching posts in indigenous communities whose languages they spoke.

Moreover, the Ministry of Education was threatening to enforce an earlier regulation that required teachers in rural schools to speak the language of their students. Attempts to enforce this in the early 1990s had been met with derision on the part of ladino teachers. Most flatly refused to learn an indigenous language. However, the climate had changed. Pedagogical materials from DIGEBI as well as those developed at the Instituto Lingüístico of Universidad Rafael Landívar had been distributed to many schools. These books were glossy and evocatively presented, but in indigenous languages. Nonnative teachers began to ask for language training so they could avail themselves of these materials.

Recent Efforts

Meanwhile, a new, more intercultural curriculum was in the works. SIMAC had been developing a new set of materials for K–12, which would celebrate the cultural diversity of the country. A new neologism project was needed to launch this new approach. In 2003 I worked with DIGEBI and ALMG on a joint project to develop the neologisms needed for this curriculum. Eleven of the twenty-two Mayan languages of Guatemala (Chalchiteko having recently won recognition) were addressed. Unfortunately, this kinder, gentler curriculum had been developed by an international panel, which, though it included Maya educators, used European and Freireian models rather than Maya ones. When the neologism team began to review the Spanish-language classroom materials of this model curriculum, we found that even the kindergarten materials were Eurocentric. One particularly telling exercise in a kindergarten workbook asked students to circle those things which were "absurd." Everything that the child was supposed to mark was something that fit in the Maya worldview: animate trees, smiling suns, and talking fires. Having asked my boss, Rodrigo Chub' Ikal, what we could do about this. I was told that we should make a list of the *impertenencias culturales.* This list finally included thirteen items, among them misspelling names of Maya lineage founders, identified in the texts as "gods," and misspelling the names of the Mayan language groups themselves; it might have grown longer, but after Chub' Ikal and I forwarded this list to the head of DIGEBI, Raxche' Rodríguez Guaján, we were told that it would do no good. The curriculum had been approved and would go forward, "impertinent" or not.

Meanwhile, the Ministry of Education went forward with plans to "professionalize" the teachers in the national schools. This was accomplished partly by in-service training, but a large part of the new approach to this training was aimed at increasing cultural sensitivity. Teachers were brought to regional centers for one day every two weeks and given tasks to explore the richness of Maya culture, as well as to develop teaching techniques for new areas of the curriculum having to do with interculturality, as well as with globalization and computation. Teachers were by and large frustrated by the poor preparation of their trainers, who often had no idea of what might be "correct" answers or effective strategies. Training in indigenous languages was limited to learning to count to three; teachers were assigned the task of finding out the rest of the numbers up to ten. Those working in rural schools could simply ask their students, but the question itself presupposes a decimal system rather than the vigesimal Maya system. This particular fault was found in the new SIMAC curriculum, as well.

In January 2003, 62,000 of the 82,000 teachers in national schools went on strike, locking their schools and classrooms to stymie scabs. Teacher demands included a pay hike but were primarily centered on the need for more equipment in their classrooms, particularly desks and chairs for the students. They also asked for the school meal program to be reinstated. Importantly, increased bilingual education and increased attention to a curriculum that respects Maya cultural patterns was prominently featured on the list of demands. After three months, the strike was "resolved" with promises of pay increases, in part tied to further professionalization, and some allocation for refurbishing classrooms and school buildings.

Also in 2003, governmental decree 19-2003 enacted the Law of Languages. This law dashed hopes of establishing one or more indigenous languages as co-official with Spanish. Rather, it affirmed Spanish as the sole official language. However, the indigenous languages would be recognized within their home areas. This recognition would entail free access to social services, to education, to security (police protection), and to justice (within the courts) in the Mayan languages. The demand for trained bilinguals in all these fields soared. The national police asked indigenous recruits to wear pins designating them as speakers of a Mayan language; court interpreters were sought after. Maya lawyers and community leaders were recruited by the Defensoría Maya, an NGO with international sponsorship working to provide legal counsel to fight cases of discrimination and to work for the implementation of consuetudinal law.

Then in December 2004, two years of intensive planning resulted in the inauguration of the Mayab' Nimatijob'al, the Universidad Maya de Guatemala. A Maya ceremony was held on Waqxaqi' Keme, December 9. The following day the university was officially launched in the Great Hall of the Miguel Ángel Asturias Cultural Center, ironic since Asturias's *licenciatura* thesis held that Mayas were the proximate cause of the underdevelopment of Guatemala and that the Indian "problem" could only be solved by importing Germanic peoples and hybridizing the stock.

During the past two years, DIGEBI had swung into high gear to produce self-taught courses in the big four Mayan languages to be supplied to school teachers in the major indigenous regions. These courses were produced on CD with an accompanying workbook and in early 2005 were distributed to the teachers along with a portable CD player. Though the pilot courses had serious problems, having been structured by a pedagogue monolingual in Spanish, before the materials were recorded in final form and distributed they were adjusted to more contextualized language use. Monolingual Spanish teachers in indigenous classrooms now had a resource to help them acquire some knowledge of the language, or as Raxche' said, at least a healthy respect for their students who can speak the language (personal communication, May 2004).

There has been steady growth in bilingual education over the past fifty years. Still, the national funds allotted to bilingual education are less than 7 percent of the education budget. In 2006 the education budget was still less than a third of that spent on defense. However, there are three interrelated and highly significant changes. First, the bilingual education now proposed is not assimilationist. The goal is not a monolingual, Spanish-speaking nation. Instead, since 2004 we have seen the first steps toward national level programs for teaching ladinos some Mayan language. Since 1995 the Universidad del Valle de Guatemala has required a Mayan language as part of the anthropology and archaelogy curriculum. The Universidad San Carlos also now requires some Mayan-language training in some programs and has its own language teaching programs. The Universidad Rafael Landívar, a leader in indigenous education since the early 1980s, continues to offer the most diverse curriculum in Mayan languages, in linguistic study, and provides the base for Edumaya, as well as producing teaching materials in most of the Mayan languages distributed free to educators. Whereas in the 1980s, ladino teachers rejected government suggestions that they learn a Mayan language, in 2003 they demanded instruction in and on Mayan languages. I have been approached to run intensive language training programs during the November break in the Guatemalan academic year. The non-Maya leadership of Guatemala now proclaims the pluriculturality of their country as a resource rather than a hindrance.

In addition to bilingual education becoming true education in two (or more) languages, recent curricular reforms seek to incorporate Maya cultural practices, cosmology, and concepts. If the actual texts fall short of the goal, they at least have set their sights on the praxis of interculturality.

And finally, Mayas are not simply on the receiving end of education or indoctrination: they are involved in the education process at all levels, from the top administrative levels of the Ministry of Education to the rural classroom. Indigenous teachers are being placed in their natal communities or in communities within the same language group. Maya schools founded by parents and teachers have managed to survive and teach across the curriculum in indigenous languages. Mayas are involved in curriculum development at the national level and in individual townships. Whereas Tecpanecos over the age of thirty recount stories of being punished for speaking Kaqchikel on the school grounds, being told that their ancestors were naked before the Spanish arrived, and learning that their "tongue" was a dialect, not a language, that it lacked grammar and had more in common with animal noises than human communication, the floats I saw of the school parades in Tecpán on July 15, 2004, almost uniformly boasted Maya themes (the exception was a float on which every child was dressed as a clown and threw candy to the crowd). Raxche,' former director of DIGEBI, summed up the advances in this way: "Before we were not even at the table, now we are" (personal communication, June 1995). For the three International Conferences on Bilingual Education that have been held in Guatemala in the past three years, Mayas are the central actors; they have made connections with their counterparts throughout Latin America. Not only are they at the table, they are "above the salt."

Works Cited

Cojtí Cuxil, Demetrio

1987   Ensayo sobre las variedades de enseñanza bilingüe: desde el bilingüismo etnocida hasta el bilingüismo etnocida. Ministerio de Educación: Guatemala.

1989   El neocolonialismo del sistema educativo gualtemalteco. Lecture to Oxlajuj Aj: Intensive Kaqchikel Language and Culture Program sponsored by Tulane University. Antigua, Guatemala.

1994   Políticas para la revindicación de los mayas de hoy (fundamento de los derechos específicos del pueblo maya). Guatemala: Cholsamaj.

Colop, Enrique Sam

1983   Hacia una propuesta de ley de educación bilingüe. Licenciatura thesis. Universidad Rafael Landívar, Guatemala.

Congreso de la República de Guatemala

1946   Ley de Gobernación y Administración de los Departamentos de la República, Decreto 227. www.congreso.gob.gt, accessed April 14, 2010.

1976   Ley de Educación Nacional, Decreto 73-76. www.congreso.gob.gt, accessed April 14, 2010.

1977   Reglamento de la Ley de Educación Nacional, Acuerdo Gubernativo 13-77, Artículo 51. www.congreso.gob.gt, accessed April 14, 2010.

Skinner-Klee, Jorge

1954   Legislación indigenista de Guatemala. Mexico: Instituto Indigenista Interamericano.

6

Democracy Delayed

The Evolution of Ethnicity in
Guatemala Society, 1944–96

RICHARD N. ADAMS

In retrospect, the 1944 revolution initiated not a democracy but rather a fifty-year transition to democracy that evolved through three revolutionary phases. These can be characterized as bourgeois, ladino, and indigenous, as each marked the beginning of serious revolutionary participation of the respective sector. In each phase the role of the United States was visible and in some manner consequential. Beginning with the revolution of 1944, the bourgeois phase established democratic electoral and administrative processes and introduced major governmental, economic, and political reforms under the presidencies of Juan José Arévalo and Jacobo Arbenz Guzmán. This saw the end of many of the abuses that had been imposed by the series of liberal dictatorships that had been in power since the reforms of the 1870s, while at the same time some changes kindled national fury against the United Fruit Company. The now well-known scenario culminated in the PBSUCCESS operation by the U.S. Central Intelligence Agency (CIA) and the fall of Arbenz in 1954. The United States chose to see many of these changes as part of an international communist conspiracy.

The ladino phase—1962 to 1968—was prompted by Fidel Castro's revolutionary success in Cuba and initiated a militant insurgency in the Guatemalan Oriente, paralleling nascent actions in El Salvador and Nicaragua. In Guatemala it triggered the introduction of the National Security Doctrine and its related counterinsurgency actions. This involved U.S. cooperation that was informed by Vietnam experiences and accompanied by highly visible human-rights abuses. I well recall, in the old Pensión Brandenburg on Avenida La Reforma, my first sight of Green Berets and realizing that the United States was once again engaged in military activities in Guatemala. The insurgency saw the bizarre emergence of weekend *guerrilleros,* often middle-class people engaged in their urban occupations during the week but leaving for guerrilla activity on the weekend. This phase ended with a bloody suppression of the guerrilla effort in the Oriente in 1968 by Colonel Carlos Arana Osorio.

The indigenous phase began with the shift of guerrilla activities to the northwest and El Petén early in the 1970s. The failure of the ladino insurgency led to the realization that the revolution would have to include indigenous political consciousness and commitment, or it would not happen. The expanding insurgent activity was aided by the earthquake of 1976, and saw the escalating counterinsurgency that exploded with *la violencia* of the early 1980s and declined gradually until the signing of the Peace Accords in 1996. The early phases saw extensive massacres, the destruction of over six hundred communities, and the flight of hundreds of thousands of refugees. While the United States officially withdrew financial support from the Guatemalan military because of human rights abuses, in fact provisioning continued (McClintock 1985: 192ff, 216) and additional military support was provided by Israel (Black 1984). This obviously reflected a contradictory situation—denying military aid on the basis of human rights violations on the one hand, and providing support for the military activities that violated these rights on the other. The continued U.S. support paralleled the assistance given the government in El Salvador and the counterinsurgency campaign in Nicaragua.

Diez Años de Primavera: 1944–54

The bourgeois phase is remembered by many as the Diez Años de Primavera (Ten Years of Spring). Democratic and capitalistic developments were energized by the emergence of various dynamic sectors that, while working for themselves, competed for control of state. Most prominent was an upper- and middle-upper-class capitalist bourgeois composed of members of both the older Spanish-Criollo sector and the increasingly active ladino population. International class lines quickly emerged to separate popular social action and governmental measures that were seen to be socialist or communistic, from the existing colonialist capitalism strongly supported by the United States. Sides were taken around *indigenista* positions that argued that the historical suppression of Indians was unacceptable (see Adams, ch. 1, this volume), but it was not for another forty years, with the approach of the quincentennial of 1492, that significant international support was forthcoming against discrimination and racist policies.

By extending the category of ladino to include criollos and *castas* (mixed-race peoples), the liberals of the nineteenth century offered some liberty and equality to the latter while denying it to the Indians. The years immediately following the 1944 revolution seemed to hold the promise of establishing a democratic regime where liberty and equality would be more available to the entire population, Indians and non-Indians alike. Because the revolution was crushed just a decade later, there followed not a progressive era of revolutionary reform but forty years of a rocky transition to democracy.

THE POLITICAL PROCESS

The 1944 revolution was an effort to displace a dictatorship that had long stifled political and economic development. Various sectors emerged to compete for political control of state policy. Most obvious was an emergent ladino capitalist middle class. Within this sector were a few who were beginning to take an *indigenista* position that rejected the historical suppression of Indians as unacceptable. Most, however, perpetuated the castelike prejudices of the previous era. There was also an immense uneducated and poor population of Indians and ladinos who were denied ready access to capitalism. They were the producers and consumers in the internal market that was necessary for development. There was also a rapid emergence of labor interests, both as political parties and in labor unions and confederations. The campesinos, both small producers and subsistence agriculturalists, also formed national confederations to push for their interests. There were no immediate signs of a pan-Indian ideology or movement.

The Roman Catholic Church that had been marginalized by the reforms of the 1870s shared the growing concern of Ubico over what it saw to be a spread of communist ideology. In the 1930s the dictator quietly permitted the church to bring additional clergy into the country and to promote the catechist movement, Catholic Action. The idea was that this would dissuade illiterate Indians who were assumed to be vulnerable to communism.

Early in the revolutionary decade the United States moved in to play what had become its classic Central American tutelary and interventionist role—to promote its own commercial and political interests—but was temporarily sidetracked when its ambassador was declared persona non grata. The socialist world established a small communist party, but its importance was magnified by the influence it had on the Arbenz government.

Collectively the Indians played almost no role in the 1944 uprising. General Juan Federico Ponce Vaides, temporarily chief of state after the resignation of President Jorge Ubico, tried unsuccessfully to use an Indian mass march on Guatemala to intimidate revolutionaries, and Chimaltenango ladinos launched a bloody massacre in Patzicía of Indians, whom they saw as opposing ladino rule and the revolutionary process. Indians around Guatemala City tended to favor the existing liberal regime as the Ubico government had given Indians some protection from local ladinos. David Carey Jr. relates how strong this perspective was in Patzicía (ch. 3, this volume). Elsewhere in the country the revolution received some support, especially where the residents felt it would better their circumstances, as John Watanabe recorded for Santiago Chimaltenango, and Christa Little-Siebold found in Quezaltepeque (ch. 4, this volume).

In discussions preparing the new constitution, Indians were regarded as a national "problem." Their social and cultural differences were seen as obstacles to national development. The assembly decided that Indians prevented Guatemala from having the cultural and racial homogeneity necessary for it to be regarded as a nation, and it should therefore be called a republic. At the core of the debate was the issue of whether these differences should allow Indians to claim separate nationalities, or whether they should be assimilated into the nation. The interesting turn in the argument was that, while assimilation was promoted, it was not conceived of as *mestizaje,* as it was in Mexico, but rather as a Criollo image now labeled as *ladino.*

In spite of the continued reign of racism, now somewhat modified through *indigenista* policies, the most important emergence of Indian democratic action was in community-level politics. Municipal governments rapidly became active and began to regain some of the controls that they had lost to ladinos in the liberal era, and specifically the power taken from them by Ubico's elimination of local alcaldes.

SOCIAL AND ECONOMIC INCLUSION

New laws, ending centuries of the forced Indian labor, introduced reforms in wages, hours of work, hiring and firing, application of justice in labor disputes, etc. A social-security system helped provide means for workers' health care and retirement. Most of these innovations were directed toward labor, but the needs of the independent subsistence farming population were addressed by forced rentals and the Arbenz agrarian reform. Labor unions were organized, and campesino leagues were started to represent the interests of the small farmers—a category that included much of the rural Indian population.

Agrarian reform in 1952 benefited some half-million people but also threatened the prevailing large landholders, a class that included U.S. interests. The reform was not, however, aimed exclusively at Indians. There was no correlation between the number of fincas or hectares expropriated, nor of the number of agrarian committees, on the one hand, with the number of Indians involved, on the other (Dirección General de Estadistica 1954; Paz 1986).

School systems expanded with social programs aimed at reducing high illiteracy rates and began raising the educational level of the entire population, as is chronicled in Judith Maxwell's review of the educational developments over the rest of the century (ch. 5, this volume). This required a new generation of teachers, new textbooks, and campaigns to familiarize parents with the importance of education and literacy. The United States promoted technical aid in agriculture, health, and education. The Pan American Sanitary Bureau was now joined by post–World War II United Nations agencies. The International Labor Organization (ILO), the Food and Agricultural Organization (FAO), and the U.N. Children's Fund (UNICEF) provided technical aid. These sources of aid were significant for the Indian population because they tended to bypass ethnic divisions and open cultural doors despite the threat to established interests.

After the fall of Ubico in 1944, the Instituto Indigenista Nacional was started with the overtly *indigenista* goal of developing the Indian population. Abigail Adams chronicles how this emerged under the direction of Antonio Goubaud Carrera (ch. 1, this volume). This was done in spite of the deeply ingrained ladino prejudices that Indians were biologically inferior and irrevocably ignorant and dirty, and that they might be "civilized" and integrated into a national society only if separated from their primitive ways. A few saw that Indian communities remained vigorous after centuries of marginalization only by retaining a strong ethnic identity and that real freedom of choice would not lead to rejecting that identity. The goals ranged from promoting assimilation to celebrating the Indian culture. The constitutions drawn up by these leaders through the second half of the twentieth century continued, however, to lean toward a tutelary role for the state.

Indian responses ranged from those of rural monolingual campesinos who avoided contact with ladinos and sought security within their community, to younger activists who were venturing into commerce and religion, and to those who thought that cultural assimilation would free them from poverty and from social and economic exclusion. In keeping with the Gramscian role for the subalterns of a class society, some of these Indians chose to keep their children from learning their Indian language, believing that this enabled them to compete better in the ladino world. A generation later, many of these children would rue their parents' choice and redirect their own children into seeking identity with the Indian community and its language and culture.

Democracy Delayed: 1954–85

These efforts to open democratic opportunities evolved within a global framework severely shaped by cold war dynamics. In 1954 the Arbenz government collapsed under a conservative coup d'état that was materially promoted by the United States, whose leaders were convinced that Guatemalan reforms were intended to bring Guatemala and (by domino-theory reasoning) the rest of Latin America within the orbit of world communism. Liberty of action and development was dealt a hard blow as agrarian reform was terminated, properties were returned to former owners, labor unions became inoperative, and most organizations that had emerged to promote democratic and class processes disappeared. Little-Siebold gives a clear account of how confused the reaction to these events could be in the countryside (ch. 4, this volume). The Diez Años de Primavera were followed by repression, faulty elections, imposed temporary governments, the militarization of the state, and thirty years of militant insurgency. The government formulated a national security policy that, with U.S. financial and military reinforcement, kept the country essentially on a quasi-wartime footing until the 1990s. The formal apparatus of democratic elections was observed, but candidates were blocked or killed, results were altered, and political activists were eliminated. Tenuous democratic processes began to return in 1985, and survived to enjoy some consolidation with the signing of the Peace Accords in 1996.

A LADINO INSURGENCY

A second revolutionary phase opened in the early 1960s with a military revolt, followed by a gradual increase of insurgent activity in the Oriente until it was crushed in 1969. In contrast to its predecessor in 1944, this was led by military rebels but, as before, it was also a totally ladino affair: Indians were ignored. Following on their military failure, ladino leaders revised their strategy and focused on enlisting Indians in the cause. They shifted activities to the northwest frontier with Mexico and the Petén and embarked on a decade of proselytizing. For the first time, non-Indians and Indians (as consciously different ethnic peoples) were joining in a political movement of national scope. Ethnic relations did not change, however, and as revolutionary action evolved over the next two decades the guerrilla organization paralleled the larger society: ladinos monopolized authority, and Indians were subordinated. Throughout the northwest, however, mobilization was being attempted within the Indian population, leading to the formation in the mid-1970s of the Comité de Unidad Campesina (CUC) in southern El Quiché. As this then became linked to the Comité Nacional de

Unidad Sindical, it evolved into a class-based organization and lost some of its specifically Indian identification.

The rise of revolutionary activity after 1960 made interest in politics increasingly dangerous for Indians. Individuals who manifested leadership abilities at the local level were commonly assumed to be communists and were killed or disappeared. Individuals sent abroad for leadership training returned to deep suspicion; those who became active political leaders—in labor organizations, as community developers, municipal mayors, teachers, or congressional deputies—or merely openly expressed dissatisfaction with the status quo became targets for assassination.

The Indian society that emerged from the 1944 revolution was still highly monolingual, illiterate, and provincial. Colonial and liberal segregation excluded them from access to consumer goods from the industrialized world, as well as from the social benefits of health services and education. Until the 1960s there was ambivalence as to what path Indian social and political development should take. The motivation of Indians to venture into the public sphere in politics began to awaken with the emergence of Indian control at the municipal level, and the effects of the slowly improving national education and health systems began to be felt.

Since political action could be dangerous, Indians moved into public activities most quickly (commerce and religion). Indian commerce had always been regionally strong, and they had long supplied foods to the capital city. Indian merchants, primarily K'iche,' spread out through the north, the Oriente, and south coast, becoming major suppliers to town markets and retail trade. Along the south coast and the Oriente, where Chinese merchants were dominant, the K'iche' replaced them. Religion, through the proselytizing of Catholic Action and the expansion of Protestantism, provided a politically safe way for Indians to take leadership roles.

With political activities blocked, another important area left open to Indian action was the promotion of Indian culture. In many Indian communities, committees founded private schools, promoted teaching of Mayan languages and culture, and the Maya religion. While much of this took place outside the purview of local ladinos, it also tended to be regarded as politically insignificant. Particularly important was Adrián Chávez's Academia de la Lengua Maya Kí-chè, which found a wide following. Among scholars, interest was growing in the better study of Indian languages, and archaeologists were making headway deciphering Indian glyphs and modeling Maya prehistory. The Proyecto Lingüístico Francisco Marroquín, and later the Academia de las Lenguas Mayas de Guatemala (ALMG), and Oxlajuuj Keej Maya' Ajtiz'iib'

(OKMA, Association for Linguistic Research), with some help from U.S. linguists, focused attention on the importance of language for the identity and continuity of Mayas. The expansion of excavations across the Petén, the identification and protecting of hundreds of sacred sites, such as Iximché, became increasingly relevant to the definition of Maya history. Of particular importance was, as related by Maxwell (ch. 5, this volume), the initiation of bilingual programs in the national educational system in the early 1980s. These developed in spite of the government's wide-ranging program of violence against the Indian communities.

The role of the Indians in the civil society was gradually growing. Domination of municipal governments by local ladinos had been interrupted in the 1930s by Ubico's displacing of municipal mayors by government-appointed *intendentes* (administrators). This weakened the local ladino power so that, following the elections of 1944, Indians found it easier to take control of municipal governments. The 1954 counterrevolution provided an opportunity for ladinos once again to assert themselves in some communities, but this was by no means universal. The new political parties early learned to choose Indian candidates for municipal office when they had a better chance to win. This was often the case in heavily Indian communities, but where local ladino control continued strong, ladinos would be chosen.

During the 1970s the Indians became salient components of the guerrilla forces; in this period the third phase of the revolution emerges. When ladino leadership turned to the northwest to seek Indian participation, they probably did not realize the degree to which they would find willing collaborators. The Indians did not become the leaders in the revolutionary action, but it must be recognized that it was then that the Indians became active revolutionaries, and in so doing provided the ladino-led military with further excuses to launch the quasi-genocidal system of massacres in the early 1980s.

With growing evidence of Indian participation in the insurgency, the government instituted community civil self-defense patrols (patrullas de auto-defensa civil—PAC). Military and PAC leaders pushed municipal authorities aside, especially Indians, further fragmenting the Indian authority system already being dissolved by the loss of local religious authority to the Roman Catholic Church. Where the guerrilla was especially active, local ladinos often became the targets of attack, leading some to abandon their homes and avoid living in heavily Indian communities. Those who returned later usually found that their former political and social dominance had greatly weakened, even disappeared.

RELIGIOUS ORGANIZATIONS

Religious organizations played an important role in social development throughout the 1944–96 era, both through changing Catholic religious practices and in the phenomenal expansion of evangelical and fundamentalist churches. In both cases, the changes reached deep into both Indian and ladino society. The Catholic Action movement, while promoted by the Guatemalan government as a defense against communism, was an effort by the Roman Catholic Church to regain control over the religious practices of Indians. The suppression of priests by nineteenth-century liberals had resulted in the Indian communities taking over their own religious affairs through control of the *cofradías* (religious brotherhoods). Orthodox clergy found this independence unacceptable and intended that the catechist movement would displace the local Indian cofradía leaders and return power to the clergy. After 1944 Catholic Action grew rapidly, splitting from the traditional cofradía practices and thereby weakening the authority of Indian elders. These new groups often took on contrasting politics. While catechists were not necessarily ethnically distinctive, they often were predominantly either Indian or non-Indian. Following the split, a more extreme Catholic offshoot, the Charismatics, emerged. Both Catholic Action and Protestant churches offered ambitious Indians paths to power that bypassed national politicians, the state, and Indian elders.

Protestant churches and Catholic Action tended to emphasize the individual. The latter focused on the individual's learning of the catechism, to be independent of the traditional cofradía structure. Protestants advocated direct individual communication with God. In both cases, the converts tended to be younger people, often better educated, less likely to be subsistence agriculturalists, more likely to be in commerce, and more economically successful. An important difference has been that the Catholic Action members tended to be politically active, whereas Protestant converts tended to be less so. The emergence of these activists exacerbated the breech between the old and the new leadership, as each tended to take different political alignments. As the conversion to the Protestant religions made the same requirements of both Indians and non-Indians, their cultures found some common beliefs and rituals. The conversions do not seem to have threatened the strength of Indian identity. Rather, it created a more diverse and stratified Indian society. In the latter years of the twentieth century, with the increasing visibility of Mayas as a publicly active segment of the population, there was a tendency in many communities for tolerance among these groups. For example, Catholic Action members have been more accepting of the cofradías, even on occasion participating in them. And a number of the wealthier Protestant sects ran good schools that were open to students without regard to religious affiliation.

THE ECONOMY

In spite of the political turmoil and social unrest, the economy experienced significant development. Underlying the political and social changes of this era, the gross domestic product of Guatemala consistently grew from the 1950s to the 1980s. Because of the vastly unequal distribution of land, the agrarian situation in Guatemala was already acute before the 1944 revolution as *minifundio* holdings were becoming too small to support a family (*minifundios* are agrarian properties greatly reduced in size through inheritance). Increasingly, the new generations were being forced out of agriculture. In 1950, 62 percent of non-Indians and 74 percent of Indians were occupied in agriculture; in 1989 this had declined to 39 percent and 69 percent, and by 2002 to 33 percent and 58 percent, respectively. Non-Indians responded more quickly to these pressures, becoming the first to see other sources of income and to migrate to northern Guatemala and then to the United States. By the 1950s the seasonal migrations to the export fincas that had been imposed by the nineteenth-century liberals were continued voluntarily because of economic necessity.

Agriculture also saw significant innovations that involved Indian subsistence farmers as well as larger-scale export producers. The technical agricultural aid that following the 1944 revolution had led to the introduction of new varieties of seed for traditional crops, but also to use of fertilizers, herbicides, pesticides, and fungicides, producing what became known as the *revolución verde* (green revolution). Because of poor guidance, many small producers found these advances illusory, but over the longer period the use of the new technologies became a regular part of the agricultural system.

Of particular importance was the impact on subsistence farmers, especially Indians, of the so-called nontraditional export crops. This began with fruits and flowers in the 1960s and 1970s, and then expanded into vegetables, of which broccoli, cauliflower, snow peas, and sweet peas accounted for almost 90 percent of the total by 1989. As was the case with the green revolution, the small producers' entry into the agricultural export market led to soil depletion and increasing concentration of land ownership, which exacerbated the effects of the *minifundio* process.

A new component of development in this era was the spread of *maquiladoras*, foreign-owned industries for export production. Many of these concentrated in the metropolitan area, but when found in more outlying areas, they absorbed an important part of the labor. Aside from their obvious economic impact, maquiladoras employed a large number of women. This had an important effect on the Indian family structures by giving women a source of independent income; it also brought them into more direct contact with workers from other communities.

Between 1950 and 1981, public-health measures led to an explosion in the Guatemalan population, which increased from 2.8 million to 6 million. The effect of this on the economy was complex. The labor force increased, but at the same time the inability to maintain an agrarian existence led to the beginning of international migration in the 1960. While at first predominantly a movement of non-Indians, with the onset of the violence in the late 1970s the annual flight north of Indians rapidly expanded.

A Second Attempt at Democracy: 1985

From 1970 until 1996 the highlands to the west and north of Guatemala City saw increasing and often intense violence that came to a head in the early 1980s, resulting in the destruction of many communities, massacres in many others, and the displacement of hundreds of thousands of people, predominantly Indians. The government's imposition of the PACs brought the vast majority of the provincial population under the direct control of the army. This exacerbated tensions between opposing factions of the local populations, as communities differed in their response to the revolutionary challenge. Many were committed to it, others sought to oppose it, but irrespective of their political ideologies, most sought to avoid direct confrontations and survive in spite of it.

Despite the violence, and perhaps in part because of it, the early 1980s saw serious signs of the emergence of democracy. It began with the decision of the state to crush the insurgency with an operation of extraordinary force. Although *la violencia,* as it became known, did not immediately achieve its purpose, it became clear that the guerrillas would never win. At the same time, members of the military, in control of the government for the previous twenty years, split over its role and sought to shed some of their power. The government underwent two coups, called for a National Constitutional Assembly in 1984, backed a new constitution together with elections in 1985, and supported a democratically elected civilian government in 1986. In effect, the military had tried to run the country in various ways for two decades, and decided that it did not like the task.

With this, more serious attempts were made to develop peace talks, and these finally succeeded in 1996. As slow as the process was, from 1986 on, the government continued in civilian hands and, among other things, succeeded in crushing an attempt by President Jorge Serrano to take dictatorial powers of his own regime and in consolidating the democratic process that continues today. More immediate in the operation of the society, 1980 also saw a severe pause in the rise of both gross domestic product and energy consumption (Maddison 2006: 515, table 4a).

THE END OF THE REVOLUTION

Although *la violencia* in the early 1980s reduced insurgent activity, it seemed to stimulate Indian leaders to organize more effectively in the promotion of their interests. From the mid-1980s until the end of the century, the government's turn toward democracy was paralleled by an increase in Indian cultural and political activity at the national, regional, and local levels. This was the first time since the colonial era that Indians ventured to promote organizations that began to accrue support across much of the Indian population. The rebellions and mutinies that dotted the colonial and liberal eras had never extended beyond the regional or local level.

For many Indians, this era of covert and military actions, from *la violencia* to the Peace Accords, were seen as an attempt at ethnocide or genocide. While it divided the Indian communities regionally, it also led to a consolidation of leadership at the national level. Agreements were reached and formalized in 1995 as the Agreement on Indigenous Peoples' Identity and Rights (Acuerdo sobre Identidad y Derechos de los Pueblos Indígenas—AIDPI). This was part of the basis of the Peace Accords signed in the next year. While many Indians supported the insurgency, many had sought protection from the army against the violence. Thus among the latter, many who witnessed the war's destruction as being the work of the then chief of state, José Efraín Ríos Montt, years later voted for his party in national elections.

THE MAYA MOVEMENT

As the violence cooled in the late 1980s, particularly active Indian organizations emerged that tended to be one of two kinds. One, the Mayanists, sought to promote appreciation of Maya culture and strengthen ethnic identity, and had often evolved out of earlier cultural committees, including the ALMG, the Consejo de Organizaciones Mayas de Guatemala (COMG), the Centro de Estudios de la Cultura Maya (CECMA), Escritores Mayences de Guatemala (AEMG), and the Centro de Documentación e Investigación Maya (CEDIM).

The second set of organizations, the *Popular*, emerged to give voice to a combined class and ethnic responses to counter the repression and violence of the war. Among these were the CUC, the Consejo de Comunidades Étnicas Runujel Junam (CERJ), the Comisión Nacional de Viudas de Guatemala (CONAVIGUA), and the Coordinadora Majawil Q'ij. In 1992 the movement received a major international boost with the award of the Nobel Peace Prize to a Guatemalan Maya, Rigoberta Menchú. Through the coming years she was to play an increasingly important role as a symbol of Indian unity.

In 1994 the efforts of Maya leaders achieved a new level of organization with the founding of the Coordinación de Organizaciones del Pueblo Maya de Guatemala (COPMAGUA), which at one point allied six organizations that included both Mayanists and *Populares*. This was relatively short-lived, and after the 1996 Peace Accords the movement began to fall apart. For the brief period of its existence, COPMAGUA marked an organizational high water of the Maya Movement. This achievement was due in some part to the fact that its construction paralleled the preparation of the AIDPI, and the signing of the Peace Accords that followed. With this the movement seemed to lose coherence. It was as if the effort had been so great that its activists needed to rest, pick up other pieces of the puzzle, and construct a new strategy.

Apart from the evolution of a Pan-Maya sociopolitical movement, the Maya migration to the United States had also taken on major dimensions by the 1990s. Large sectors of the new generation of Mayas were going north for varying periods. Aside from changing the gender composition of the Guatemalan labor force, perhaps the most important impacts of this movement were the injection of U.S. currency into the provinces from expatriate Guatemalans and the urbanization and internationalization of the younger generation. Remittances grew steadily, increasing from $302 million U.S. in 1994 to $563 million in 2000, then rocketing to $2.5 billion in 2004, and were growing more rapidly than national exports. About 20 percent of the Guatemalan residents who are benefiting are Indians (OIM 2004: 25).

A final and fundamental dimension of the changing situation between Indians and non-Indians in Guatemala derives from the differential emergence of the demographic transition. The ladino death rate had already fallen to 15 per thousand by the late 1950s, whereas the Indian rate did not reach that level for another twenty years. By 1995, both had declined to less than 7 per thousand. The ladino birth rate declined from 45 per thousand to about 33 between the early 1970s and 1995, whereas the Indian rate had declined only from 45 to 43 per thousand. The natural increase of the ladino population thus exceeded that of the Indians until sometime in the 1970s or 1980s, when the advantage shifted to the Indians.

The government censuses have not reflected such a change in the relative percentages of the two populations over this period. Rather, the Indian population has remained around 42 percent since 1964. The failure to record an Indian increase may be due to two processes: a higher rate of international emigration for Indians than for non-Indians; and assimilation, whereby people born Indian do not claim this identity when responding to the census takers.

Reflections

By the end of the twentieth century, the goals of liberty and equality were far advanced in comparison with the status in 1944, but the past half century has also pointed up more clearly vast areas of inequality and lack of liberty. In the regimes that followed the 1996 Peace Accords, Indians were invited to fill some ministerial level posts and were slightly more represented in congress. Unfortunately, some of the promised advances were neutralized by failures to follow up on proposed and enacted legislation, especially those designed to implement the Peace Accords, and by continuing intense corruption that derailed many legitimate programs.

Moreover, gains in the democratic process have been slow to reduce prejudices and racist predispositions that lie deep within the historical experience of both non-Indians and Indians. Along with the Peace Accords, various U.N. conventions were signed in the 1980s and 1990s aimed at eliminating discrimination, but until 2005 little had been done to expose abuses publicly as practices that the state and all Guatemalans needed to openly address and combat. An important exception occurred in April 2005, when Menchú won a landmark case in the Guatemalan Constitutional Court against five defendants for discrimination based on congressional decree 57-2002 (in appeal as of this writing).

Significant gains in democratic processes in Guatemala began with the revolution of 1944. Until that time, many liberties and equalities were enjoyed only by specifically segmented minorities of the population—the Spanish and Criollos until 1824, then only literate Criollos and Castas as ladinos until 1944. Since that date, in comparison with the inertia of previous eras, there has been real progress, but inequalities abound in all dimensions of the social system. Nevertheless, slow though it may be, multiculturalism is becoming a working reality in Guatemalan life.

The effect of the 1954 U.S. intervention undoubtedly contributed to delaying the emergence of democracy in Guatemala. In view of this, it is perhaps worth noting the similarities between the Guatemalan case and that of Iraq a half century later. In both, a world situation was perceived to threaten the sanctity of the United States—then communism, now terrorism. In both, a single leader in a small foreign country was alleged to have threatened the physical security of the United States—then Arbenz in Guatemala, and later Saddam Hussein in Iraq. In both periods the U.S. regime was composed of a Republican elite heavily influenced by U.S. business interests—then a northeastern establishment together with United Fruit Company (McClintock 1985: ch. 10), and later the intimate involvement with the oil establishment by friends of the George W. Bush administration. The solution in both cases was the preemptive use of force and massive psychological campaigns of defamation to get rid of the bad eggs. In both there emerged within the existing government bureaucracy a small cluster of political analysts and advisors, insulated from and intentionally marginalizing the existing security organizations, that focused on a strategy for the destruction of the regime in question—then the PBSUCCESS team within the CIA, and in the Iraq case the Office of Special Plans within the Pentagon. In both cases the plans were kept secret from the U.S. State Department and many other departments. These cells ignored the problems that would follow the proposed intervention, and set the United States on programs of regime destruction with no sophisticated and clear plan as to how to put Humpty Dumpty back together again. While Guatemala and Iraq were obviously different cases in major dimensions, the composition of events leading to the interventions are unpleasantly parallel.

From the standpoint of the U.S. government, operation PBSUCCESS was apparently singularly successful. For Guatemala, the outcome cannot be so readily characterized. The U.S. intervention was a material factor in, among other things, the destruction of an agrarian reform that directly prejudiced the welfare of some half million people, perhaps 20 percent of the population, thereby contributing to an era of continuing poverty (Schöultz 1983). It promoted the military domination of the government—which Eisenhower warned against. It provided the basis for thirty years of civil war, which eradicated over six hundred villages and displaced or killed hundreds of thousands of civilians. All development efforts, specifically foreign aid programs operated under clear constraints against programs—specifically the agrarian reform—that the entrenched oligarchy and U.S. policy makers regarded as "communistic." This was in spite of the fact that many studies, including those of the U.S. Agency for International Development (USAID), clearly identified the problems of poverty and land deprivation (Hough 1982), and that the United States had overseen such a program in Japan in 1947 with considerable success.

The government's failure to prepare a sophisticated series of alternatives to deal with the consequences of the destruction of the Iraqi regime and infrastructure is disturbingly evident in the daily newspaper articles that began in 2003 and continue today. It took half a century to bring into public light the documentation of the U.S. Department of State and the CIA stemming from the Guatemalan intervention (U.S. Department of State 2003, U.S. CIA 2003). Those fifty years were not enough for the U.S. government to learn from the failure of U.S. planning and policy in Guatemala. Because of that inability to learn, the problems the United States faces in disengaging from Iraq are incomparably greater than those faced in Guatemala.

Works Cited

Black, George, in collaboration with Milton Jamail and Norma Stoltz Chinchilla
    1984   Garrison Guatemala. London: Zed, in association with North American Congress on Latin America.
Dirección General de Estadistica (DGE)
    1954   Censo Agropecuario—1950. Boletin Numeros 49–50. Guatemala.
Hough, Richard, et al.
    1982   Land and Labor in Guatemala: An Assessment. Washington, D.C.: U.S. Agency for International Development.
Maddison, Angus
    2006   The World Economy. Vol. 2: Historical Statistics. Development Centre Studies, Organization for Economic Cooperation and Development, Paris. P. 513, table 4a.
McClintock, Michael
    1985   The American Connection, Vol. 2: State Terror and Popular Resistance in Guatemala. London: Zed Books.
Organización International para las Migraciones (OIM)
    2004   Impacto sobre impacto de remesas familiares en los hogares guatemaltecos, año 2004. Cuadernos de Trabajo Sobre Migracion.
Paz, Guillermo C.
    1986   Reforma agraria. Guatemala: Cuadro E.
Schöultz, Lars
    1983 Guatemala. In Trouble in Our Backyard. Martin Diskin, ed. Pp. 180–181. New York: Pantheon Books.
U.S. Central Intelligence Agency (CIA)
    2003   CIA Historical Documents on 1954 Guatemala Coup. Two compact discs. Washington, D.C.: Central Intelligence Agency.
U.S. Department of State
    2003   Foreign Relations of the United States, 1952–1954: Guatemala. Washington, D.C.: U.S. Government Printing Office.

Epilogue

The October Revolution
and the Peace Accords

VICTOR D. MONTEJO

TRANSLATED BY ABIGAIL E. ADAMS

In this epilogue I highlight certain striking similarities and differences between the October Revolution of 1944 and the Peace Accords, signed December 29, 1996, by the Guatemala government and the guerrilla forces, to end a civil war that lasted almost thirty-six years, nearly to the end of the twentieth century.

Perhaps the most relevant similarity between these two sociopolitical movements is that these are the only *total social phenomena* of the entire history of Guatemala from independence in 1821 until 2005. The idea of a "total social phenomenon" refers simply to those events that affect all levels, aspects, and stages of transformation of society. These events affect the foundations of society in a way that more superficial events of a reformist nature do not; these latter influence isolated areas such as the arts and education and do not result in a structural change of the entire society. The October Revolution, that is, the sociopolitical movement that includes the governments of Juan José Arévalo and of Jacobo Arbenz Guzmán, was aimed at the complete transformation of Guatemalan society, from its foundation to its less tangible aspects, such as individual behavior, thought, and morality. It must be noted that the foundations of a democratic climate of civic values, open-mindedness, and respect were laid during the Arévalo administration, most certainly due to Arévalo's own professional development and personality, but also due to the global and national climate (the end of the Second World War and the fall of the Ubico dictatorship). Building on that foundation and Arévalo's achievements, Arbenz undertook a radical transformation of Guatemalan society.

He proposed, to begin, moving beyond the feudal stage in which society was stagnating, most evident in agricultural labor relations, in which agricultural workers were considered part of real estate, tied to an inhumane way of life. He proposed moving the nation to a capitalist stage, which he announced in his inaugural speech as the democratically elected president and which he demonstrated in his outlined platform for government. The platform consisted of the following four basic objectives: agrarian reform; construction of the Atlantic highway; construction of a major port on the Atlantic coast, the Port of Santo Tomas; and construction of the Jurun Marinala hydroelectric station. The first objective was, and remains, indispensable for changing the land tenure pattern responsible for the medieval stagnation of our society, the unjust distribution of wealth that affects all of society, in which the vast majority of the population live in inhuman conditions while a minority enjoys an enormous proportion of the national wealth. Arbenz proposed the last three objectives as the means of breaking Guatemala's dependency and alienation, in which the foreign monopoly of electricity, transport, and exports exercised political and economic control in the country.

The 1996 Peace Accords also aimed at a radical transformation of the nation, with one additional element that was not expressly included in the platform outlined for the October Revolution: the reclaiming of the basic rights of Guatemala's indigenous peoples and respect for their non-Western cultures. They constitute more than half the population and have demonstrated a power of cultural resistance and strong identity that forms the image of the Guatemalan people, including, in a dialectic sense, ladinos and even the upper classes of society.

It is true that neither the October Revolution nor the process of the 1996 Peace Accords realized fully their objectives. But somehow the October Revolution and Peace Accords resemble each other, in terms of the obstacles confronting each movement, and the opposition raised by almost exactly the same national and international actors. In the first case, opposition grew to the extreme of an invasion that was rationalized within the framework of the cold war, and involved the open participation of the U.S. CIA and banana monopolies who counted U.S. State Department officials among their stockholders. In both cases, Guatemala's army and economic elite took a decisively reactionary posture.

It is only fair, however, to point out that both cases opened a progressive dialogue around the national reality and a widespread fight to improve the living conditions of the most marginalized peoples, those who suffer social exclusion, poverty, and appalling misery. It is also important to point out that the position of the international community toward the Peace Accords is not exactly the same as its position in 1954, when the Arbenz government was overthrown, because, among other factors, multilateralism is more consolidated now in the framework of international affairs.

There are many other factors that could be interpreted as similarities and differences at the same time, in a comparison of these two moments. For example, the cold war was the background for 1954, during which a radical anticommunism predominated across the Western world, and during which the most heinous dictatorships were automatically included, such as those that proliferated across Latin America. Currently, in the name of maintaining individual and national security under the real threat of international terrorism, governments can suppress those marginalized majorities whom the elite and powerful try to stigmatize and identify unjustly as terrorists.

Furthermore, while the 1950s were marked by the polarization between the communist nations of Eastern Europe and the Western world, today, the tendency toward globalization creates a system with contradictory consequences that negatively affects indigenous peoples and the marginalized majorities of the Third World.

Another of the numerous differences between the two events that concern us: despite today's relative progress in the areas of education, health, and technology, we have not addressed the basic needs of the vast majority or overcome social inequality, or, therefore, achieved the objectives set in the Peace Accords. Instead, we have witnessed the excessive and predatory commercialization of education, health, and other essential services that the majority of our people lack.

There are other factors of social disintegration that affects the very nature of the Peace Accords. Violence, criminality, runaway consumerism, narcotrafficking, the growth of fundamentalist sects, the corruption of unions that destroys the humanitarian and egalitarian nature of this social instrument, and internal and external migration (primarily to the United States), all of which are closely linked to the conditions of misery in which the majority live.

Finally, there are two fundamental factors that fit reasonably within a systematic comparison of the 1944 October Revolution and the application of the 1996 Peace Accords. The first is the emergence of increasingly solid ethnic identity among the overwhelming majority of peoples of pre-Hispanic origin, which still occupy extensive territories of the American continent. After the fall of Arbenz, and for a period following, the government implemented an indigenist policy aimed at the integration or the ethnocentric incorporation of indigenous peoples, a policy that was developed, whether in good or bad faith, by professionals such as Antonio Goubaud Carrera.

Guatemala's indigenous peoples became aware of the general problem of ethnicity and its consequences, such as the discrimination they suffered, the deep and prolonged exploitation to which they had been subjected for centuries. They also began to value the intrinsic force of their thousand-year-old cultures, and their capacity for resistance against cultural attacks, some bloody and others peaceful, that aimed to rob them of their identity just as they have been robbed of their lands, resources, and fair pay for their labor that has been so decisive in the entire history of the national economy. The potential of indigenous cultures, their social organization and physical resistance, has been taken advantage of, first by the Roman Catholic Church and then by the guerrillas—organizations that initially consisted exclusively of ladinos who held the misshapen ethnocentric ideas that are common in that segment of society. Indigenous people, nevertheless, succeeded in strengthening their cultural and organizational potential, albeit at a great cost in blood and suffering, and in strengthening a social and cultural resurgence in which the Maya, Xinka, and Garífuna people join. The Pan-Maya movement is without doubt a great movement that gains strength, breadth, and bearing every day in the life of Guatemalan society. Although similar movements are emerging in other American countries, particularly in the Andean world, there is no doubt that our particular movement is directly related to the 1944 October Revolution and to the 1996 Peace Accords in Guatemala. And these movements continue, despite the stigmatization and open opposition of those sectors of society whose interests and positions are threatened.

The other fundamental fact that I referred to earlier is the concomitant rise of social sciences that, in the case of Guatemala 1944–54, took an integrationist position, complicitly and indirectly rationalizing the status quo, in contrast to a committed and critical social sciences, in which indigenous people have stopped being simple objects of study and are now active subjects, interested in their own cultural identity, in their basic rights, and in a future of full equality and social justice.

Contributors

ABIGAIL E. ADAMS
Central Connecticut State University,
Department of Anthropology

Abigail Adams's research and teaching interests include relations between North and Central Americans, Maya cultural revitalization, Guatemala's civil reconstruction, and environmental anthropology. She has studied how and why a U.S. evangelical mission and a Q'eqchi' Maya congregation built the largest evangelical church in Guatemala at the height of that country's civil war. Before her academic work in Guatemala, she worked in Central America as an editor and freelance writer covering health care, the region's civil wars, women's economic development issues, and the international debt crisis. She earned her doctorate from the University of Virginia, a master's degree in Latin American Studies from Stanford University, and an undergraduate degree from Haverford College in biology and anthropology.

RICHARD N. ADAMS
University of Texas at Austin (Professor Emeritus),
Department of Anthropology

Richard Adams has been the president of both the American Anthropology Association and the Latin American Studies Association and was the director of Latin American Studies at the University of Texas. He was also a fellow of the John Simon Guggenheim Memorial Foundation in 1973. He is considered by many to be one of the most influential social scientists to have worked in Guatemala. He is the author of numerous articles and books on social change and ethnicity in Guatemala including *Crucifixion by Power: Essays on Guatemalan National Social Structure, 1944–1966* (University of Texas Press, 1970) and *Etnia en evolución social: estudios de Guatemala y Centroamérica* (México: UNAM-Iztapalapa, 1995). He was the 1998 recipient of the Kalman H. Silvert Award, the highest honor given by the Latin American Studies Association. His email is rbadams80@yahoo.com.

DAVID CAREY JR.
University of Southern Maine,
Department of History

David Carey Jr. is an associate professor of history and women's studies at the University of Southern Maine. He holds a doctorate in Latin American Studies from Tulane University. His publications include *Our Elders Teach Us: Maya-Kaqchikel Historical Perspectives : Xkib'ij kan qate' qatata'* (University of Alabama Press, 2001), *Ojer taq tzijob'äl kichin ri Kaqchikela' Winaqi'* (A history of the Kaqchikel people; Q'anilsa Ediciones, 2004), *Engendering Mayan History: Mayan Women as Agents and Conduits of History, 1870–1970* (Routledge, 2005), and *Latino Voices in New England* (State University of New York Press, 2009, edited with Robert Atkinson). He is currently working on a manuscript about gender, ethnicity, crime, and state power in twentieth-century Guatemala.

CHRISTA LITTLE-SIEBOLD
College of the Atlantic

Christa Little-Siebold is a Guatemalan anthropologist and an adjunct professor of anthropology at the College of the Atlantic in Bar Harbor, Maine. Her research over the last fifteen years has been in Quezaltepeque, where she has focused on the politics of identity in eastern Guatemala. She has taught courses on campus and for the college's international studies program in both Guatemala and Mexico's Yucatán Peninsula. When she is not doing research and teaching she dedicates herself to her family and community on the coast of Maine.

JUDITH M. MAXWELL
Tulane University,
Department of Anthropology

Judith Maxwell's work focuses on discourse primarily within Mayan languages, particularly those of the K'iche'an and Q'anjob'alan families. Questions that interest her within discourse are canons for artistry, encoding of cultural constructs, mechanisms of coherence, coreference and tracking, knowledge and belief states, presuppositions, creating and indexing societal relationships, alignments, animacy hierarchies in relationship to syntactic and pragmatic structures, and masking. She also works with contemporary language issues: the processes of standardization, language maintenance and shift, bilingual and multicultural education, and issues of language, identity, and authenticity. Her work with colonial manuscripts, primarily in Kaqchikel and Nahuatl, explores issues in language change, borrowing and restructuring in conditions of contact, and lexical embellishment and shift. Her books include *Kaqchikel Chronicles: The Definitive Edition* (University of Texas Press, 2006, translated with Robert M. Hill II) and *Of the Manners of Speaking that the Old Ones Had: The Metaphors of Andrés de Olmos in the TULAL Manuscript* (University of Utah Press, 1992, with Craig Hanson).

VICTOR D. MONTEJO
University of California at Davis,
Department of Native American Studies

Victor Montejo is a Jakaltek-Maya scholar from Guatemala. After being forced to flee Guatemala in 1982, he enrolled in graduate school, receiving his doctorate from the University of Connecticut. He is professor of anthropology and Native American studies at the University of California at Davis, and he has lectured in the United States, Central America, and Europe. He has written several books, including *Testimony: Death of a Guatemalan Village* (Curbstone, 1995), *The Bird Who Cleans the World and Other Mayan Fables* (Curbstone, 1995), *El Q'anil: Man of Lightning* (University of Arizona Press, 2001), *Voices from Exile: Violence and Survival in Modern Maya History* (University of Oklahoma Press, 1999), and *Popol Vuh: A Sacred Book of the Maya* (Artes de México y del Mundo, 2005, with Luis Garay). At the time he gave his keynote address for the conference from which this volume stems, he was Guatemalan secretary of peace in the Oscar Berger administration and member of the Guatemalan National Congress.

JUNE C. NASH
City University of New York (Distinguished Professor Emerita),
Department of Anthropology

After earning her doctorate in anthropology at the University of Chicago in 1960, June Nash was a visiting professor at the State University of New York at Albany and held a distinguished visiting chair at the American University in Cairo and the University of Colorado. She retired in 1998 as distinguished professor emerita at the City University of New York, Graduate College. Over her lengthy career, she has been a fellow at the Bellaggio Center of the Rockefeller Foundation and a William Allan Neilson Professor at Smith College. Her research has been funded by the National Science Foundation, the National Institute of Mental Health, the Social Science Research Council, the National Endowment for the Humanities, and the MacArthur Foundation. She has received the Franz Boas Distinguished Service Award, the highest honor give by the American Anthropological Association (1995), and the Kalman H. Silvert Award, the highest honor given by the Latin American Studies Association (2004). Over the past fifty years, she has written or edited fifteen books and dozens of articles on the anthropology of work, human rights, social movements, gender, resistance, and globalization. She has also been involved in the making of two films.

TIMOTHY J. SMITH
Appalachian State University,
Department of Anthropology

Timothy Smith did his undergraduate work at Tulane University and received a doctorate in anthropology from the University at Albany, SUNY. His research interests include violence and conflict, development, citizenship and the state, multiculturalism, linguistic revival and change, environmental conservation, and grassroots indigenous politics in Latin America (Guatemala and Ecuador). His research and writing have been supported by Harvard University, Columbia University, the U.S. Fulbright Program, the National Science Foundation, the U.S. Department of Education, the U.S. Department of State, the Institute for Mesoamerican Studies, the Institute for Mesoamerican Studies, and the Roger Thayer Stone Center for Latin American Studies. He is coeditor of *Mayas in Postwar Guatemala:* Harvest of Violence *Revisited* (University of Alabama Press, 2009, with Walter E. Little) and has published in *Ancient Mesoamerica, Reviews in Anthropology,* and the *Journal of Latin American and Caribbean Studies.* He is currently working on a manuscript about indigenous identity and electoral politics which is the culmination of a ten-year study of indigenous municipal governments, citizenship, alternative democracies, community development, and protest in Guatemala over the past 150 years. It focuses on the history of Kaqchikel Maya governance and leadership in Sololá from 1490 to 2009. He served as associate director of the Center for Latin American and Caribbean Studies at the University of Illinois at Urbana-Champaign from 2004 to 2005.

Index

139–140, 141, 154; reduction of, 144–145. *See also* armed conflict; civil war; Guatemalan Armed Forces; *violencia, la*

Handy, Jim, 9, 40n3, 107, 112n9
Hersch, Burton, 56
homogeneity: ethnocide and, 59; Guatemalan national identity and, 11, 18–19, 25, 26, 28–29, 37, 137; ladino desires and, 87; racial, 27
Honduras, 23, 52, 99, 100
human rights, 68, 70n6, 76, 90, 93, 129, 135,
Hussein, Saddam, 148
Hutchinson, R. C., 55

Imparcial, El, 27, 28, 41n24, 42n26, 53, 85
indígenas, 74, 100, 101, 117
indigenista philosophies, 4, 11, 18; Arévalo and, 6–7; Castillo Armas and, 153–154; Goubaud and, 17–48, 138; Mexico and, 57, 58–59; Ten Years of Spring and, 135–137. *See also* bilingual education
indigenous peoples, 36, 37, 39; agrarian reform and, 26, 108; Arbenz and, 7, 77, 106; Arévalo and, 7, 92; assimilation of, 78, 117; Castillo Armas and, 99, 110; Catholicism and, 9; discrimination against, 26, 153; education and, 5, 51, 115–133; in ethnographies, 50–52; girls and, 127; globalization and, 153; guerrilla movements and, 135; historical perspectives of, 11–12, 73–98; identity of, 4, 10, 61, 100–102; ILO and, 24, 129; labor and, 35; land tenure and, 35; languages of, 59, 118–133; Mexican, 57–59, 61; missionaries and, 6; municipal leaders and, 99–100, 106–110; October Revolution (1944) and, 87; Peace Accords (1996) and, 152; political and cultural awakenings of, 7–8, 12, 18, 26, 36, 104–107, 134, 154; religion and, 51; research on, 42n36, 64, 154; state relations and, 27–28, 74, 76, 84; teachers and, 120, 129, 132; violence against, 18, 59–60, 63–64, 81. See also *indígenas*; Maya Indians; pan-Mayanism
indio: as derogatory term, 89, 92, 101–102; as racialized identity, 101–102; as self-description, 101
inequality, 9, 59, 147, 153
Instituto Indigenista Nacional (IIN):

Arévalo and, 7, 116; Goubaud and, 11, 17, 19–20, 23, 27, 30, 36, 39; ladinos and, 38; October Revolution (1944) and, 18, 24, 37–38, 138; Vela and, 23, 27–28. *See also* indigenista philosophies
International Labor Organization (ILO), 24, 129, 138
Iran, 1, 68
Iraq, 147, 148, 149
Israel, 135
Iximché, 141
Izabal, Department of, 126

Jehovah's Witnesses, 51
Jutiapa, Department of, 111n6

Kaqchikel Maya Indians, 76–93; *caudillos* and, 93n4; discrimination against, 133; Goubaud and language of, 19, 23, 31; language of, 117, 118; neologisms of, 127–128; oral histories of, 11, 73–93; PRONEBI and, 119; Townsend and, 120; Ubico and, 74, 93n2
K'iche' Maya Indians, 22, 30, 31, 41n25, 50, 140
Kissinger, Henry, 68

labor: abuses, 54; coffee and, 35; debt peonage and, 9; ethnicity and, 7, 87, 137, 154; gender and, 146; *maquiladoras* and, 143–144; October Revolution (1944) and, 136; in the post-coup (1954) era, 139, 140; protest, 60; religion and, 4; Ten Years of Spring and, 9, 136–137, 151–152
ladinos: as agents of the state, 74; agrarian reform and, 9, 107; alliance with Maya Indians, 12, 35, 81, 102–103, 107; Arbenz and, 8, 83; Arévalo and, 106; the coup (1954) and, 9; demographics of, 146; domination of Maya Indians by, 6, 35, 86, 103–108, 139, 154; ethnicity and, 29, 36, 101–103, 136–137; Guatemalan Armed Forces and, 110, 141; higher education and, 124; historical perspectives, 73; identity of, 36, 50, 100; IIN and, 38; indigenous view of, 76, 77, 81, 84, 89; the media and, 80, 85; Mexican, 57; MLN and, 111; municipal governments and, 8, 81, 106–107, 137, 141; in El Oriente, 100, 110; Patzicía massacre

The University of Illinois Press
is a founding member of the
Association of American University Presses.

———————————————————

Composed in 10.5/13 Adobe Minion Pro
with Meta display
by Jim Proefrock
at the University of Illinois Press
Manufactured by Cushing-Malloy, Inc.

University of Illinois Press
1325 South Oak Street
Champaign, IL 61820-6903
www.press.uillinois.edu